Drain ThatPain

Joanna Cameron

This book is dedicated to all people in chronic pain. May you find education, inspiration and the imagination to let it go here...

*Drain ThatPain** is a holistic energy therapy for chronic pain elimination using active imagination. Many people have expressed relief from chronic emotional and physical pain. Individual results may vary. However, you should not use this book to diagnose or treat any health issues or for prescription of medicine or other treatment.
You should always consult with your healthcare professional.
If you are taking medication, you must be in contact with the provider to come off it safely.

Drain ThatPain has been used to eliminate pain with the following:

Allergies
Arthritis
Brain fog
Carpal tunnel syndrome
Chronic fatigue syndrome
Complex Regional Pain Syndrome (CRPS)
Chronic back, neck, shoulder, arm,
knee, leg, wrist and hand pain
Depression
Emotional pain
Fibromyalgia
Grief
Irritable bowel syndrome (IBS)
Lupus
Migraines
Phantom limb pain
Post Traumatic Stress (PTS)
Psoriatic Arthritis
Rheumatoid arthritis
Sciatica
Shingles
Spinal stenosis
Temporomandibular jaw syndrome (TMJ)
Tendonitis
Tinnitus
Torn meniscus
Trigeminal neuralgia

Chapter	Page

Thank You to our Book Contributors

Elizabeth Cameron

Ian Cameron

Amanda Dobra Hope

Randi Light

Angel Metatron

I. Musluer

Carol Robertson

Becky Shanks

Dominique Shipstone

Nikola Tesla

Benetta Wainman

Rhona Wands

Jim Ward - Author

Robin Williams

Becky Willoughby

Amanda Wright

Fact or Lore?

Mythology or History?

Goals

1)   That this book educates and inspires you to let go of emotional and physical chronic pain and that you, as the reader/listener will join us in that shared intention. Let's imagine a world free of chronic pain! Even if you don't believe — can you just intend?

2)   That you gain an understanding of yourself as an energetic spiritual being who is here on earth to love, laugh, thrive, and live out your dreams, and to know that those dreams really can come true.

3)   That you strive to live the life of your Soul's highest intention — a life of service to humanity; to be a force for good and to let your joy ripple out into the world.

4)   That this book helps you to listen to your Soul and believe in messages from the unseen. The question is not whether your Soul talks, but rather, have you opened up your intention and awareness to listen?

5) That this book inspires you to be compassionate to yourself first. To love yourself, care for your body, move for the joy of it, go inside and feel the connection of your heart and divinity, to meditate daily, and to enjoy the moment.

6) That you commune with nature and take time every day to meditate (at least five minutes) and renew your connection with your higher self while enjoying the freedom of letting go of your ego (earthly self).

7) That your first thought every morning when you wake up is gratitude! Gratitude! We have one heart and together we really can bring heaven to earth.

All that is really required is an open mind!

CHAPTER 2

Dharma

Dharma is the Buddhist word for purpose. To be in dharma is to have found your path — your spiritual purpose in this world. I am in dharma! Having made the documentary *Drain ThatPain* and written the majority portion of this book — I've never been so focused or indeed happy in my life. Is everything perfect? No. Like you, I have challenges, and at times they have seemed daunting, but I know I am surrounded by love and am well protected.

You are at your best in life when you are in love. Nothing increases your energy vibration more than being in love. You can be in romantic love with a person, your spiritual journey (dharma), your newborn baby, or all three at the same time! When you are in this state, oxytocin courses through your system and the world is better. The moment shines!

When I started this journey in June 2017, I knew I needed to make a documentary and write a book. Experiencing people letting go of chronic pain was so joyful — the best experience ever! I've always known that I was a messenger, a teacher — now a healer with a special message.

You can let go of chronic pain permanently

Before, I started this journey, I could never have imagined how wildly exciting my life would become! When you are on purpose, you see signs along the way. Maybe a book falls open at the right page with a nugget of information that you need. No matter the sign, the important part is that you learn to trust it. It's a wake-up call. It may be showing you something that you need to focus on or to just relax into. When you are in dharma, in purpose, the right people show up at the right time, with the information you need.

I'd like to introduce you to a few of those people to illustrate how being in dharma has helped me to receive what I need at just the right time, as well as how it all connects!

Hillary Evans

Hillary Evans, a Charleston hypnotherapist, asked me if I would connect with one of her clients, Cliff, who was suffering with dreadful pain in Myrtle Beach in July, 2017. Cliff is now pain free and is a featured case study in the *Drain ThatPain* documentary story line. We will take a deeper look into Cliff's story later in this book.

Jim Ward

I've known my author friend, Jim Ward, for a while. We met because we take our morning swim at a similar time in a local pool. Traveling back and forth to

Joanna Cameron

Nashville and other filming destinations has kept me out of town a great deal. Now, as I am back home and writing, I am reminded of Jim's stories and talents. He is America's great storyteller. Jim tells swashbuckling stories, page turners set in the Amazon jungle, high seas and many exotic lands! Here's what's interesting about my friend, Jim. He does not know where his books are going. Why? Because the characters begin in his imagination, while their lives unfold before our eyes.

Jim, dazzler to extreme measures, is not only a great storyteller, but he also examines the native Amazonia tribes, including the Kogis and the Yanomami. His fascination means that he goes the extra mile on research and even reads the local Brazilian newspapers in Portuguese. Jim, like me, is also clairvoyant (sees clearly). This means he has opened up his intuition and can receive messages from the unseen. We all have this power, it's simply a question of being quiet, setting the intention, and listening. A person using this type of process to receive a message is called being "in channel" or being "a channel" in spiritual circles. As Jim has studied these tribes, as well as sometimes being their channel — they sometimes come to him with messages. My synchronicities with Jim run deep, as you will see throughout the following examples. But first, let me give you a little background on the Amazon tribes that Jim covers in his stories.

The Kogis are the Dalai Lamas, the supreme channels of the Amazonia people, and the original divine tribe. Residing on a sacred mountain, Sierra Nevada de Santa Marta in Columbia, their world is about harmony. This unique tribe has a dreamland climate! Because of it's distinctive latitude, there are an equal twelve hours of light and twelve hours of dark everyday, year-round! Life expectancies top one hundred years for these peace-loving people who treat each other with love and respect, and who know how to extend life because of their contacts with the unseen.

The word Kogi means jaguar! The ancient native shamans teach that the Big Cats came first, long before humans. The Kogis venerate and hold the jaguar in highest esteem. If you watch the Kogis climb tall trees in a matter of seconds, you can tell they learned from the jaguar!

The spiritual practices for the Kogi are based on *Aluna* — simply enlightenment and that thoughts create reality, which has both a physical and a spiritual essence.

The Kogi *Mamos*, who serve as tribal leaders, are carefully chosen children brought up in caves without light for the sole purpose of raising them to become spiritual leaders of the tribe. This is the greatest honor and privilege. Without light, these children learn how to become aware of the unseen, communicating first with their namesake, the jaguar. Of course, these channeling abilities have been used to share information from the spirit world between ancient tribes as well. Incredible as it may seem, the

Kogis also exchange information with the Aboriginal people in Australia.

Messages from Kogi channels that Jim has received indicate they are extremely worried about Mother Earth. There is a particular sacred seashell, used to make a potion for man/woman relations which has changed in structure. Also, for so many other reasons, including massive islands of plastic — the oceans are in trouble.

I channel Nikola Tesla, and I feel it like a tug in my spine, which I call the "Tesla tug." The tug is an awakening for me to slow down the moment and really look at it, really feel it. These messages can be as random as when I see a certain number plate.

I never know when it might happen, and at times it totally surprises me. Sometimes I write in these moments, and I will actually be sharing a Tesla channel in a few pages. Sometimes, however, it is a message for me to do something right at that moment. This was one of those times.

As I was writing one day, I leapt up intuitively and went to the back of my closet and found my father's cardigan. It even had his name, Ian Cameron, on a name tag in it. I then hurriedly got in my car to take it to Jim's house, three hours ahead of our appointment, because I realized that Tesla wanted Jim to have the cardigan. My intuition tells me that my father's energy, which is in his cardigan, is protecting Jim. As you read on, you will find that my father was and still IS (though deceased) a very protective, loving man.

In 2012 Jim met a young man named Niko at a local gym. He was a loner from Greece — a handsome, fit man, who spoke with a Serbian accent. He was in the Washington, DC area Special Operations with the Greek government, and he was in enormous pain. He told Jim that he was having a kidney transplant surgery in the States, and it was likely that he would not survive. He instructed Jim to call his phone number in a year. Dutifully, Jim did as he was asked. There was no response — Niko had died or rather transformed. When I brought Jim the cardigan, and Jim figured out that Niko was indeed Nikola Tesla! It shook him, too! We know the same Soul!

Another exciting thing that connects Jim's work to mine is that the Amazonia tribes have ways to remove pain. In the Yanomami tribe, the Paje (pronounced Par-jay) is the healer. The ceremonies involve a specific fire (the Yanomami make 15 kinds of fires), and pain elimination has its own fire. It's an epic event, done with intention, drama, and for the Yanonami, lots of tobacco smoke.

Pain Elimination is NOT something new. We are instead opening up our awareness to relearn something we already knew.

CHAPTER 3

Multi-dimensional Child

I've always felt that I was a multi-dimensional being. And why wouldn't I? I mean – think about what happens when you sleep — you go somewhere else and then have convenient amnesia when you wake up, right? You must have been somewhere else during that time. I believe that you are off visiting other dimensions. I've always liked being in my own creative space. As a child, I played with puppets. They each had their own personalities, and I was absorbed in my own world. I remember watching people speak, and it was as if their mouths were moving, but I was not hearing the words — just constantly day-dreaming. My husband might tell you that nothing has changed!

Apparently, I had whooping cough as a baby, and my parents thought that I had died. My blond curly hair became straight hair and waited till my teens to curl again. By the age of eight, however, I was aware that I had something different in my body — a growly entity. In current times it would be called an elemental. It was scary — like having a sadistic exercise coach! My sister and I had heavy twin beds in our Victorian home in Shawford, Hampshire, and it would demand that I lift the bed many times. It was loathsome, and I don't use that word idly. I was afraid that it would devour me and I would lose my Soul — myself. Desperate, I finally plucked up some courage and talked to my father on our way to go fly fishing on the River Test. He pulled the car off to the edge of the road. Standing by the side of the road, he asked me to point to where it was inside my body. I pointed to my stomach. "What does it look like?" he asked, and I replied, "Ink!"

With authority, he said, "Pull it out of your body!" and he purposefully started waving his arms about as we both went through this imaginative exercise, arms waving in the air in the idyllic English countryside! I remember the entity leaving and feeling its absence. The color changed to divine light in my stomach, and I knew it was gone.

It's a memory I treasure with my father, and I'm so grateful. I know what he did was totally intuitive and came from a place of love, I'm so grateful that I was able to watch and experience love conquer fear at such a young age.

What the experience has also taught me is that I am attuned to those energies in others. I feel the presence of entities in people and in animals, and when called upon to help, I can do that.

CHAPTER 4

A Message from Robin Williams

The Law of Attraction works in the unseen the same way that it works on the Earth — you attract into your life "like-minded energies."

I adore Robin Williams! A particular channeled conversation between Robin and me went something like this:

Me – I don't think you can laugh and have pain at the same time. Your way worked! How's life on the other side? You are ON, and you always are/were in front of people!"

Here's what I heard:
"Hello from somewhere else, also known as heaven! I know you are thinking this is crazy-ass "woo woo" but there is no other side, backside, or otherwise — it's all now and I am here in your thoughts to tell you that all my life I feared that I would die slowly, lose my skills — just gradually fade away, upset my family, and become a burden; not be able to communicate with my toy soldiers, and most of all causing you pain by watching me fade away. For you, my family and fans, I didn't want you to remember me that way.
"Actually, I caused my own death! Yes, by my own

hand, but really by my own thoughts. By fearing it all my life! I know now that I created my worst fear. But actually, death does not exist. It's transformation into a rainbow-feather-bed, Baby! It's floating into puffy-white-clouds in baby-bliss and oneness — Kum Ba Ya is optional! There are angels with wings, and trumpets, and some with both — not your regular pajama party! Everybody belongs and even laughs at my jokes! Yours too! So my message is to forget that fear stuff! Live one moment at a time, there is nothing to fear. Heaven is all around you! In fact, if you look carefully you can see me sending you love hearts and kisses coming out of the puffy clouds, the trees, buildings; everyone and everything. Oooh — I'm all a buzz."

CHAPTER 5

Nikola Tesla

Throughout the making of the *Drain ThatPain* documentary, there were so many synchronicities. The most amazing was the 1111, numerology as it's called. We filmed in Nashville on November 11, at the Holiday Inn Express at 1111 Airport Center Drive, which is just one of many examples. What is it about the number "1?" The energy of the number one suggests a first step which symbolizes new energy. Parallel 1's suggest a path. Several 1's can look like a gate. Numbers, patterns of nature, and their inherent creative energy are all terribly important — especially to Nikola Tesla.

I'm always grateful for these messages of alignment from Mother Nature, and never more so than when I met Nikola Tesla through a license plate, and then had an introduction come my way a few days later through a psychic medium.

1111T1

As bizarre as this may seem, a medium who I had never met before was compelled to contact me and introduce me to Nikola in the unseen. The question from Nikola that came through the medium was, "What is the significance of the New York Post building?" I replied, "The hexagon and other sacred symbols — shapes in the art nouveau architecture." Yes! That's Nikola! What a privilege.

A Message from Nikola Tesla

"Ladies and Gentlemen — Hello to you from a time ago! Might I introduce myself? I am the infamous Nikola Tesla, whom Einstein called the smartest man alive, which is a compliment when you consider the source. I know what you are thinking — what about Thomas Edison? Well that fellow was a shyster. My alternating current (AC) at Niagara should have allowed for the general public to have free electricity rather than Edison's direct current (DC). However, he knew the powerhouse money families: Rockefeller, Carnegie, Vanderbilt, Guggenheim, JP Morgan, Ford, and others. Avarice was the name of their game. These people wanted to charge you for energy that I knew could be free. I was always working on my experiments and didn't focus on money for myself. However, I do hold three hundred patents of motors, generators, alternators, wireless frequencies, and am the inventor of radio. In 1926 I predicted a pocket size wallet that would allow everyone to communicate freely and wirelessly, and you know this handheld thing, I believe!

"I've always known my brain was a receiver. After I recovered from an illness/death experience as a youngster, I spent a scheduled part of my day in meditation, which brought me peace and information. So as the inventor of radio, let me tell you boldly that you can tune into a higher frequency. Your level of awareness is a choice. In the same way with radio now, I believe there are lots of channels, so you have a choice what to receive. It is the same with your brain. You just need to train it. There is a seeming modern day malaise of anxiety and depression, best taken care of by breathing and meditating and connecting to divinity. This will give us the greatest secret of all — the sacred code of the Universe. And, of course, it's mathematical.

"Many people feel that I was obsessed with the numbers 3,6,9, and I was! I still am! Yes, I walked around buildings three times before I entered them and ate with eighteen napkins. It worked! And it has also worked for Buddhists, who walk three times clockwise around the Stupa, their shrine, and the pinnacle of the Stupa spire is enlightenment! Now that I've got your attention, I'll tell you why that matters in a later chapter when we talk about higher dimensions within the Universe.

"Ladies and gentlemen, until then I'll leave you on this note. Soon, you will be able to recharge your wireless processor wallet (now called a cell phone, I believe) seamlessly without plugs, as you take a walk, perhaps with it in your vest pocket!"

CHAPTER 7

Becky Willoughby

My friend and guide, Becky Willoughby, is an internationally recognized psychic medium, medical intuitive, pain eliminator and clairvoyant (actually she has all the "clairs.") That means she is not only clairvoyant (clear seeing), but also claircognizance (clear knowing), clairsentience (clear feeling), clairaudience (clear hearing), clairangency (clear touching), clairsalience (clear smelling) and clairgustance (clear tasting). Becky's psychic and channeling skills enable her to find lost pets. Amazingly, she gets in touch with the pet's essence or higher self. You can read more about Becky's work in her book, *Switch on Your Psychic*.

A Message from Tesla via Becky (unedited)

"Healing starts at a microscopic level, every cell can restructure itself. Just like plants, we grow and adapt. We have the ability to shed and restructure ourselves.

Our blood cleanses the body and oxygenates it.

We all have the ability to heal ourselves at a certain level.

Our eyes take in information which can alter the

healing process and hinder it sometimes.

The information we receive is based on our comprehension.

Intention can also alter cells in our body and DNA, with the best intention being to always put our best foot forward to strive forward within ourselves.

Planning our journeys can hinder us and restrict at times, go with the flow of what we receive and feel is right within us, never doubt yourself, always trust and you will be right."

My advice is to trust your own mind, to know that's your own thinking. Never doubt yourself! Our minds can be comprehensive entangled webs within us. Don't get caught up in webs. Be free. Don't allow others to alter your being. You are a unique being — a sentient of one. Go with the flow in harmony, for harmony has a wonderful vibration. Just like music, harmony heals too.

Harmony is sacred. It is to be at one with ourselves. When we're in harmony we play music within to our cells, our body, and our mind .

Always be — just be. Stay safe with love.

CHAPTER 8

It's All Energy...

"All that we are is because of what we have thought." — Buddha

So here's a new thought — I believe that in 10 years or less (let me not impose any limits) we will look back and say, "You know the medical profession used to give people awful drugs and even do exploratory surgeries to manage chronic pain, all because they thought the cause of chronic pain was structural."

The cause of chronic pain is negative (often repressed) emotions that cause stuck energy that can manifest as pain. Loving intention quite simply can allow these emotions to drain away.

Drain ThatPain is Pain Elimination, not Pain Management. It's a New Mindset!

It's easy to look at our bodies as finite structures. I think we are more akin to weather patterns, energetic and ever changing. This book challenges you to look at everything as energy. This includes pain, love, and all of your thoughts. Imagine your body as an energetic receiver which not only receives energy from the ends of the Universe, but generates energy, and eliminates unnecessary energy as well. Drain ThatPain is the release of unwanted energy. Your brain is the command center — a beacon, a processor, or a lighthouse in the dark. It receives information from both your body and the Universe. Chronic pain, anxiety, and depression are messages that you need to listen to your body. Go inside in order to feel and learn something that will integrate mind, body, and Soul.

This book is written with the intention that you will let go of pain. Be the change that you want to see in your life! Understand that you are here to thrive, laugh, and love. Let the world be your oyster!

The goal is to educate and inspire you, dear reader, to imagine the life of your dreams as you help your family, your community, and our planet Earth!

Exercise – Feeling Energy in Your Hand

Let's do an exercise as you are sitting there (but not while driving a car). Squeeze your left hand into a fist and keep reading. That feeling as you squeeze your hand is a feeling of focus on the hand. You may feel warmth, your fingernails in your palm, or your knuckles tighten. Now, how do you feel that in the rest of your body, I wonder? One thing you may notice is that your hand feels stuck in that clasp.

Joanna Cameron

Now, breathe in — hold it for a second, and then re-lease that hand as you breathe out and place it over your heart. Now your heart feels warmer and loving as you feel your heart energy going out into the world while your breathing slows. You feel peaceful and in the moment, connected and open.

This is how letting go of pain feels in your body. You let go of feeling "in the clasp" and having the expectation of pain. You go from feeling stuck to feeling connected with yourself and others.

If you are reading this in emotional pain, I need to tell you that this moment will pass. Say out loud to yourself right now, "I wish I was grateful." Say it again, "I wish I was grateful — I wish I was grateful." After a few repetitions, I bet you are smiling. But hold that thought — you now feel grateful as well! The feeling comes because of the power of the resonance in that word.

The root of joy is gratitude. Gratitude is the buffer against pain. Waking up feeling grateful is the greatest gift. Every morning, make a choice to get out of bed with love and gratitude. If you don't feel grateful then say, "I wish I was grateful" until you ARE.

CHAPTER 9

Your Chakras

I was in Mexico many years ago receiving a massage and my therapist asked, "After the massage would you like me to balance your chakras?"

I looked mystified, so she replied, "It's an energy healing. You'll feel great!" Who could argue with that? The massage was wonderful but then the words I never like hearing were whispered in my ear, "The massage is over. Please could you turn over." As I laid there with my eyes closed, nothing seemed to happen. Out of curiosity, I peeked. She was standing there waving her arms over the base of my spine. I relaxed.

When it was over, I felt strangely energized and at peace with the world. Apparently my third eye chakra, the center of my intuition in my forehead, was blocked. In Eastern belief, everything is energy and

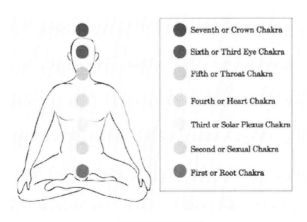

Seventh or Crown Chakra

Sixth or Third Eye Chakra

Fifth or Throat Chakra

Fourth or Heart Chakra

Third or Solar Plexus Chakra

Second or Sexual Chakra

First or Root Chakra

this life energy is not only the cosmos, our higher self, and our spiritual world, but also our God, our families, our pets and our planet.

Negative emotions block the flow of energy and cause the chakras to shrivel or stop spinning.

Let's look at the chakras and understand more about the stuck energy or rather negative emotions that adversely affect the way you feel. Start with your divine chakra at the top of your head which spins with a bright white. This is your connection to cosmic energy, and it is blocked by ego and earthly attachments.

Your pineal gland in the center of your forehead is your connection to your intuition. When you tell yourself lies — "I'm not good enough, I don't belong..." — your chakra, which is normally purple may change color and stop spinning. The answer is, of course to love yourself first.

Lies again, self-berating talk block your throat chakra that deals with what you say and your verbal expression. Your word must be your bond for this to spin with an azure blue. Now let's move to your heart which spins with the color green, and it is blocked by grief and sadness. It's literally "opening up your heart" to love.

The solar plexus chakra is in your stomach, your gut and is the center of your power, and it spins with the color yellow. It is blocked by shame. Hanging onto childhood shame or lies you tell yourself blocks your power.

The sacral chakra is your sex organs — it's about pleasure and creativity. It spins in orange. If you feel guilty that you don't measure up in some way, then this chakra may shrivel and change color.

Your root chakra at the base of your spine spins with the color red, and it is all about elimination. When you are operating from a place of love and confidence — life flows. However, when you live in fear, this chakra may change color and shrink.

An understanding of the concept of the chakras is important. Bathing/showering, being out in nature, exercise, laughing, or imagining rainbows of light going through them all help to balance your chakras. We do the latter (rainbows) in a Drain ThatPain session.

To protect yourself from any negative energy you may encounter, imagine a yellow bubble of gold light surrounding you.

Let's feel those chakras in your body. Again, it's about relaxing and understanding the feeling in your body as you go inside. Let's connect up your divinity or crown chakra with your heart chakra.

Joanna Cameron

Exercise to Feel Your Heart and Crown (Divinity) Chakras Combine

With one hand touch your heart, breathe in, and stay in that moment. As you feel your heart begin to warm, you may feel a tingling in your head. I will always feel it in the top of my head as a reminder that my heart, my Soul, my essence — must stay in contact with my divinity.

Next, touch your crown chakra with your other hand as you keep your heart and your divinity connected. Then, memorize the first question and wait for your heart to respond.

Close your eyes and ask...

1) Is it OK for me to let go of emotional pain?

Acknowledge the feeling in your body...

Now open your eyes and memorize the next question and close them again and ask....

2) Is it OK for me to forgive myself?

Acknowledge the feeling in your body... Open your eyes and memorize the next question and close them and ask ....

3) Is it OK for me to acknowledge that "We" (all of us) have one heart in this world?

Acknowledge the feeling in your body... Open your eyes and memorize the next question and close them again and ask....

4) Is it OK for me to love myself first?

Acknowledge the feeling in your body.

Some people feel warmth, tingling, or hear/feel their heart beating! Notice how hyperaware you become as you listen to your body — now that's inner power! I frequently see colors.

Did you know that there is more information going from your heart to your brain than from any other organ in your body? It does make sense though. Think about it — if your heart feels good, generally speaking your life feels good.

Learn to listen to your heart, and feel the warm, tingly sensations in your body. Understand that your thoughts and feelings become physical within your body.

CHAPTER 10

Your Body-Mind

Subconscious Mind = Unconscious Mind = Body-Mind

Did you know that it is believed that you are only about 5% conscious? That means that you are 95% unconscious. What a relief! It would be impossible to be fully conscious of the trillions of processes happening in your body. Your faithful body-mind breathes for you, digests your food, and integrates your brain functions while you sleep.

Your unconscious mind or body-mind is simply what you are not conscious of right now. You may have just blinked your eyes, but you weren't aware of it until I brought it to your conscious attention. The conscious mind can only take in about seven bits of information at one time, whereas the unconscious mind is unlimited. Consider an iceberg, where just the tip (conscious mind) protrudes above the surface but there is so much more (unconscious mind) underneath!

Your body-mind is constantly changing and evolving, just like your own thoughts, imagination, and experience. You are like a planet of 50 trillion cells, spinning around the sun in a constant energetic exchange with the

stars, the moon, yourself, infinity, and beyond!

Your thoughts are certainly not limited to the physical constraints of your body. They resonate to the end of the Earth and beyond!

I talk about the body-mind in every session of Drain ThatPain. I often compare it to a seven-year-old child. It wants to play, imagine, and have fun. However, its main function is to protect you. During a session, we work directly with the body-mind and set up signaling using the head-nod. People instinctively nod when they agree with you. Most people will readily nod their head when I say that pain is a message. If you are the client in a Drain ThatPain session, know that it is best to close your eyes so you feel the head-nod and don't verbalize it.

Signaling With the Body-Mind

If I were performing a session with you, I would ask you to relax, close your eyes, and take a couple of deep breaths. I would then explain that I want the head-nod to come from your body — so don't speak, but rather just give me a head nod for "yes." In simple terms, I would ask you, "Can your body give me a signal for 'yes'?" I would then wait until the nod comes from the body and I know that you feel it. When I can tell that you are feeling it, I would confirm that to you by saying, "Great. That nod was different from your conscious nod." Next I would explain to you the difference between old pain and new pain. I would tell you that an example of new pain could be pain from an accident, and it is asking you to take action. Chronic pain is different; it has been around in some form for a longer period of time. After I explain the difference I would confirm that your body-mind understands by asking you, "Does your body-mind know the difference between old pain and new pain?" After I get a definitive head-nod or "yes" from you, I would then ask you directly, "Is it OK for you to let go of this discomfort consciously and be aware of it unconsciously?"

In every Drain ThatPain therapy session, I signal with your body-mind to make sure that you understand the difference between new pain and past pain. The body's primary function is to protect you, so it would be counterintuitive for it to leave you unprotected. It is the compassion you have for yourself. Your genuine self-love and desire to move on allows the pain to drain. After all, it's only stuck energy — "poison" that keeps you stuck in painful thought processes. You are here to experience love and see beauty everywhere. Quite simply, love is a higher vibration than fear.

Further into a Drain ThatPain session, and once you are dissociated (looking from afar) from any troublesome events, I will ask, "Was the origin of the negative emotion underneath the pain before or after your birth?" At this moment I may snap my fingers as I don't want you to go conscious and think, but rather just to let that information come from your unconscious body-mind. Don't be surprised if you burst out "Before!"

What happens in these situations is that though you may not consciously believe that to be true, in your body-mind or unconscious mind, you understand.

The cause of chronic pain is negative, repressed emotions and limiting decisions that manifest as stuck energy within the body. Know that your loving intention is enough to let the pain go — even if you don't believe. I like to say to people, "I know you may not believe but can you please intend to let it go, and wake up in the morning feeling fabulous!"

CHAPTER 11

Love Rules

"The most important decision we make is whether we believe we live in a friendly or hostile Universe" – Einstein

Love is so powerful that it is has even been proven that loving thoughts can quell the fearful ones. Love IS that much more powerful than fear. In the early 1980's at the height of the Middle East war in Lebanon, it was hypothesized that if enough people collectively meditated and radiated peace at the same time the progress towards peace would be facilitated. What happened during that time supported this theory. It was recorded that the more people that meditated in Jerusalem each day, the more desperate acts of terrorism measured by deaths and other parameters decreased. Subsequent experiments continued to statistically confirm that 10,000 people radiating peace could temper the negative energy of one million.

Healing the World or bringing "Heaven to Earth" involves more and more people going inwards, discovering their own divinity, and projecting that love out into the world.

The message is such good news! It means that your positive thoughts are at least 100 times more likely to prevail. The system is rigged in your favor. You are destined to succeed!

The Maharishi effect (1% effect) named after Maharishi Mahesh Yogi for the transcendental meditation, appears to point to the power of the collective unconscious — and is also in agreement with Ayurveda or Vedic Science. Creating a "protective bubble" in the collective unconscious allows a community collective resilience in the face of war and other disturbances. This is analogous to The Meissner Effect in quantum physics, whereby the highly coherent resonant state of a superconducting metal resists any external magnetic field from affecting the internal integrity of the superconductor.

It is estimated that there are over 7 billion people in the world. If only 70 million (1%) of them meditated every day — wars would stop and people would reach out to help others. There would be no more hunger or slavery, and endangered species would thrive. Renewable energy would be the norm, and the plastic bags in the ocean would disappear! Let's dream about that world and know that our combined loving thoughts can make that happen.

CHAPTER 12

The Statue in the Stone

Now, to look at the Sistine Chapel
Is to gaze at a labor of love
Awed indeed by its color, magnificence
And creativity
We think about the artist
The hours of work
Michelangelo lying on his back
Far in the air
A belief in his ability
To create a masterpiece
No plan on paper
But perfect in the mind's eye
And how did he decide, I wonder
Which piece of stone
For his statue of David
An adherence to the Laws of *Disegno*
Or divine creation
He knew without a shadow of a doubt
That the sculpture of David
Was already there
Set inside the stone
But not just this stone
There is a beautiful sculpture
Within every stone
Just harder to find within some
More chipping is required

Bit by bit to find the core
Sloughing off bits not needed
But it is there
A wonder to behold
Frozen music
Every note personified
And humans you know
Not so long ago
Looked for the "Soul"
By weighing the body
Before and after death
And did they find the "Soul"
You may ask
For just like Michelangelo
We needed to chip away
Bit by bit
Discarding what is not needed
To find the warm good part
Of the heart of the matter
Always there
In spite of a few hard knocks
And when I look at
The statue of David
I notice that David's hands
Are larger
Out of proportion
To his body
Like those mirrors at fairs
That distort the body
And make you laugh
Because human beauty

Is in the eyes of the beholder
So maybe it is OK
To get to know yourself
Today
Whatever your shape
Because you ARE that person
That you said you wanted to be
Now
Aren't you
So you can just relax
And allow your dreams to take hold
Because it is all there
And that is something
That is set in stone
And Michelangelo
Dare I say it
Is a Soul man
A creative genius
With an angel in his own name

CHAPTER 13

Your Soul

Higher Self = Soul = Higher Power = God = Divinity

As a child I remember watching a bird, caught by our marmalade cat, take its last breath in my hand. When the bird's eye was half-closed, the bird's Soul left and I felt that change in the palm of my hand. The life force left the bird's body – I saw it first in the eye, followed by a temperature change in my hand. I instinctively knew that this was death/transformation. Maybe you too, dear reader, have a similar memory. It's the miracle of life and the transition which death creates. The Soul is the peanut inside the shell. When the Soul leaves, the earthly body dies but the spiritual one lives on.

You can see a person's Soul by looking into their eyes! I believe that we are spiritual beings living here in time and space in our "meat suits." We are Souls, spiritual beings, having everyday human experiences — and we choose to be on Planet Earth.

Our "meat suits" are entirely made of energy, although they appear to be solid because of the primitive nature of our sensory organs. That energy, that life-force — your thoughts, desires, and yes — your intention, purpose are what

**attracts other people, subsequent events,
experiences, and even Unicorns that become
your life adventure!**

I love the expression, "Mind, Body, and Soul." If you
want something with your mind, body and Soul, then
you really want it! The Soul is the spirit, the life force
within you that provides direction — a path. You simply have to listen and allow it to invade all your senses
with its magic! Trust it! Surrender to it! Let it guide
you! It is your inspiration — literally 'in spirit' form
— your enthusiasm, your radiance, your excitement,
your spontaneity, your laughter, your joy, your
dreams, your "falling in love," your compassion, your
gratefulness, your love of life, and also that pain.

**You must trust your Soul (which includes
your infinite connectivity and creativity)
in order to move forward as a co-creator
in the life of your dreams!**

For me, any discussion of chronic pain involves the
Soul — the Spirit within you! Pain is transformative.
You have chronic pain because there is something
that your Soul needs to learn. When you learn it,
you'll be able to move on. The learning is often as easy
as owning your own power — to simply intend to let
it go within your body because it's really just stuck energy. I believe it's better to learn it now than to keep
creating the same situations in numerous lifetimes.

I understand you may not believe in a Soul that continues after death. If that is true for you, is it still pos-

sible for you to read/listen to this book and get out of pain? Absolutely!

The Soul is believed to exist in the body behind the eyes in the middle of your forehead, deep inside your brain in the pineal gland — often known as the third eye. The Ancient Egyptians as well as many other cultures have long revered the third eye as the "all-knowing Soul," and the center of your intuition. Your intuition is so important. Your hunches are real! You may know that feeling of "goosebumps" or a "shaking" of your spine. Feel it, act on it, and follow it! It's the Universe's way of telling you that you've got this — you are on your path!

I believe that we all have a path — a spiritual journey. Our Souls have chosen to be on this planet, on a mission to learn something, to remember something we already know, and to help others.

Have you ever looked at a baby and said to yourself or even out loud — "There's an old Soul?" The baby appears wise beyond its years — like a Buddha baby! Let's hope our Buddha baby takes the conditioning of the first seven years of life in his/her stride and retains the ability to emanate love, wisdom, power and reverence on her/his journey through life, just as the Buddha did.

It's a powerful thing to be both driven by a spiritual path and humble at the same time. Accomplishing this allows you to live a life of

Joanna Cameron

purpose. What is your purpose, I wonder? Have you had a spiritual awakening? Is that pain in your body a spiritual longing?

CHAPTER 14

Elizabeth Cameron

If you've seen the documentary, *Drain ThatPain*, I talk at the beginning of the movie about my mother, Elizabeth Cameron. She died of cancer when I was twenty four years old. The last fifteen years of her life were very difficult for everyone around her, but mostly for her! As I mention in the documentary, — "It's hard to watch someone in pain." I know this first-hand as I chose to look after her and give her hospice-type care the last few months of her life. Looking back, I am very grateful for the intimate time we spent together, as well as for the love, inspiration and fun that IS my mother's Soul.

I was brought up in England and Scotland and graduated from the University of St Andrews BSc Honors in Zoology. After that, I moved to Salt Lake City, Utah as a research assistant, studying cell biology at the University of Utah and becoming an avid skier in the Utah powder snow! I moved home to Scotland for the last six months of my mother's life, and she died in 1975.

Returning to the States at 24, after my mother's death — I became a student tour operator bringing American students to Washington DC (where I moved a few years later), New York and Boston for educational spring break tours. It was an amazing experience. I love the special energy of teenagers, working with teachers, and the Broadway shows! I loved this business so much that only after forty three years am I finally discontinuing to head these tours. As of this writing, the first year I will "retire" from giving these tours is 2019.

For so many years, living and working in downtown Washington, DC just blocks from the White House, I never had any sense of my mother. She was a WREN, a volunteer women's navy recruited organization and she worked in Washington, DC at the end of the second World War. Everybody worked in the war effort. Elizabeth Cameron did morse code communication between the White House and 10 Downing Street. I didn't know a great deal beyond that about her work, but

I do remember her telling me that it was very hot and sticky (British phrase for humid) and, of course, there was no air conditioning beyond electric fans at that time.

She had a huge revelation at the end of the war. There had been frantic morse code communication right before the first atomic bomb, and she had had no idea what was going on. "That's what it was!" she said after the bomb exploded over Hiroshima.

Fast forward to 2014. My husband, daughter, and I were invited to a fabulous, formal wedding at the Willard Hotel, right next to the White House in Washington, DC. As we entered the Willard Room, Bach's Arioso in G was reverberating through the room. I was gobsmacked, frozen in my tracks, and overcome with joy! Yes, my mother had requested that same music at her funeral! I looked at my husband, Harvey, and my daughter Chelsea, and said, "My mother is here!" I knew that to be true with every molecule in my being! That was and still is one of the happiest moments in my life! My mother loved getting dressed up, organizing parties and yes — making an entrance! The day after the wedding at the Willard, there was a morning brunch. When we arrived, Harvey said to me, "Go check on Mum in the Willard Room!" When I went toward the Willard Room (which was not being used for the brunch on this day), the door was open and I was able to enter into the quiet and peaceful darkness. I knew I was not alone as my mother's Soul permeated every atom and quark in this enchanting room. I was overjoyed again with the same knowing that was more than omnipresent — it hung in the air!

Fascinated with my Willard experience, I did research on the Willard Hotel. In the 1940's it needed structural work and was vacant. However, the government was desperate for space during World War II and apparently it was decided to open up the Willard Room for communications. I got it — Elizabeth Cameron had worked there! Goosebumps!

Amazingly, every time I've returned to the hotel, the door to the Willard Room is always open — and yet I'm told it's always locked! Let's remember it is arguably the most beautiful, authentic, and elegant function room in Washington, DC!

At the same time my family was invited to the party at the Willard Hotel, I was working as a comedy hypnotist in the college and military markets, and I also had a practice as a clinical hypnotherapist. I loved my career — entertaining and making people laugh, as well as helping clients to stop smoking, let go of weight, etc. However, I decided I also wanted to open up my intuition and learn more about my spirituality. I've never considered myself a religious person (though I do love amazing cathedrals, organ music and some of the traditions of the church), but in this case, I was looking for a more universally spiritual experience.

Let me indulge you for a moment about my wonderful father. Ian Cameron was an atheist who liked to sing Christmas carols rather loudly in church! He was a very funny man, and he loved to tell jokes. He would start laughing hysterically in the middle of telling them, and though we were laughing as well, he never got it that we were all laughing at him! Joy and laughter were the way in which he approached his life. He once told me, "You know, Joanna — I've been married three times (he had a short rebound marriage after my mother died), and two out of three were really happy! I beat the odds!"

What I learned from the Willard experience was there was no reason to fear death, because there is no death — only transformation. We are all infinite beings. I'd always intuitively believed in the Soul and its infinite nature, and this moment was the "icing on the cake!" I felt it...

Of course, I want to die peacefully — we all do. I believe the Soul continues, and that you can even get another chance of life on this planet if you choose it. It's all about your spiritual journey of learning.

CHAPTER 15

Anxiety

The pain (or rather the "noise" as I heard it) for me was anxiety. In order to heal it, I needed to surrender and learn to be in the "moment" in my life. I was always thinking I should be in another moment, as if that moment was somehow better. It was a way of belittling my own thinking.

As my own story continued to unfold, I felt the need to connect with other people who were also interested in the spirit. To address that need, I started a Facebook group called Hypnotic Intuitive Women and connected with some of the greatest healers on the planet. Coincidentally during that same time, since I've always loved to teach, I decided to train others in confidence building and "stage hypnosis" all over the world. What I discovered along the way was that I was not just teaching stage hypnosis, but I was learning about spirituality (just as I had intended) from some of these amazing healers! I began my travels in Rome, and then traveled widely throughout Europe, the United States, Canada, and Australia. Along the way, I studied with some very talented people including: Nicky Alan, Steven Blake, Peggy Bonfield, Michelle Braun, Rick Collingwood, Beryl Comar, Lorraine Gleeson,

Marina Makushev, Theresa Micheletti, Helen Mitas, David Snyder, Brenda Thompson, and Becky Willoughby. I also became a Reiki Master, studying with my friend Shelly Rose in Wales.

"Anxiety is a message from your unconscious mind that you need to focus on what you want." – Tad James

If you are focused on what you are missing in life, then you are projecting into the future what you don't want. More than that, anxiety robs you of the present moment. Remember that you get in life what you focus on.

Opening up your awareness to the present moment actually relaxes you and allows information from the life force, your spirit — your higher self to enter your awareness. It really is the secret! Your perception changes when you get into a relaxed, receptive state. When you relax, get out of fear, and dream — the magic happens!

Anxiety and depression are a function of fear. I experienced anxiety as a feeling of "another shoe was about to drop." The cup was half empty, not half full. When I understood that the thoughts in your life do become things, I made a conscious decision that I was not going to tolerate anxiety. And I knew I had changed as I now notice when I feel calm in a situation, which in the past would have felt like a hot flash — a panic attack. And certainly, I have virtually removed hot flashes from my life. You can let go of fear by understanding that in an infinite world where there are infinite possibilities, dreams really can come true! Anxiety and depression disappear when you allow yourself to believe and trust in the unseen.

"You're never given a dream without also being given the power to make it true" – Richard Bach, *"Illusions"*

I've always believed in an infinite world full of infinite possibilities, and the Universe has provided. Many of my dreams have come true. Just like yours! In the past, I felt it was the mechanism ("how" dreams come true) that I needed to study. Actually it was the "how" that was the root of my anxiety. I needed to learn to detach from the "how," and instead have trust and faith that it would happen. If you have read, *The Spiritual Laws of Success*, by Deepak Chopra, you will understand that the Law of Least Effort is how nature is able to work with effortless ease.

Just as the sun rises every day and bamboo shoots always appear in my garden on May 15, the same is true for you. It's a principal of nature, of harmony and love. What you desire is already within you, so let go of the 'how" and detach from the outcome — the Universal Law of Detachment.

Our ego-self that can only see the physical realm often has the need to control and micromanage situations, rather than let go, detach, and let the Universe work its magic. To follow the Universal Law of Detachment is to learn to trust your Soul (which is the Universe itself). I keep a copy of Deepak Chopra's *Spiritual Laws of Success* by my bed, and at times I just open it. In that moment, I know what I need to remember will be on the page I'm looking at.

Since stress can in many ways be related to anxiety, we should also take a look at the adrenal glands, which sit on top of the kidneys. When you are anxious and under stress, the body acts by sending messages through the autonomic nervous system to the adrenal glands to prepare the body for "fight or flight" by releasing the hormone, adrenaline.

The adrenal glands can essentially be worn out with chronic anxiety. The way that you perceive pain is directly related to the health of your adrenal glands. If the adrenal glands are strong, your body has an easier time making the pain go away.

Exercise to Remove Anxiety

Focus on a spot in front of you, at least twenty feet away, or even outside the window perhaps. Now open up your peripheral vision, while keeping your head still. Take a deep breathe in — 1,2,3,4 and now out — 1,2,3,4.

Feel it in your heart chakra.

When you open up your peripheral vision, you get out

of tunnel vision, which accompanies anxiety. Your peripheral vision also connects you with your spirituality. In some cases, people actually see Souls "fleet by" in their peripheral vision. This is one great reason to feel grateful — knowing there's always a bigger picture.

Now put your hand over your heart.

Read this sentence, memorize it, and then close your eyes and say it.

"With every breath I take, I become more and more grateful and joyful. I know that loving energy can bring heaven to earth."

You can't have anxiety and gratitude at the same time — your body doesn't do that. So choose gratitude! Your Soul, by nature, is always aligned with the Universe. You are the Universe because it's what you create.

How did it all begin — A big bang perhaps? Love is the most powerful force in the Universe. The Universe began with love. We are all love at our core, for it is the original vibration. We are all God particles.

When you align your physical body with your Soul as well as the Universe, you become a co-creator of your fabulous life — where dreams absolutely do come true.

So I say, why not dream really big dreams? Go for it! To Heal the World is to bring Heaven to Earth.

CHAPTER 16

Grief

"Your friends will know you better in the first minute you meet than your acquaintances will know you in a thousand years" - Richard Bach

Kristi's Story

I met Kristi Judy in Las Vegas at a conference where I was teaching in August of 2017. We met each other in the hallway outside my classroom. The bond was instantaneous — a loving, laughing, spine-tingling knowing in each of us that we have known each other for many lives.

Kristi said that her Soul gave her more than a nudge that day and literally pushed her into my classroom.

At the end of the class I did a group session of Drain ThatPain and asked all those who wanted to let go of pain to stand at the front of the class. I prefer to perform the drain while people are standing if possible. There were approximately eighty people in the class, and twenty five of them came to the front. During a session, pain is measured in numbers with 0 being no

Joanna Cameron

pain and 10 being the highest. I asked everyone to say their numbers out loud and then asked all those with numbers higher than 8 to stand near me, as I needed for them to be in close to my heart energy. Kristi was one of the people standing close to me, and it was obvious that she was in emotional distress. Here is the amazing part. She was so ready to let go of that pain, she was able to let it go in four minutes! Here's the even better part — I never even knew the reason for her distress until later in the day.

The fact that we can do Drain ThatPain without needing to know the details of someone's pain is wonderful. It shows respect to the Soul, feels safe to the body, and therefore allows it to set the pain free.

After the class I learned that Kristi was in grief after the loss of her teenage son, Zack. She told me that after the session she felt free to be Kristi again. I love our friendship. We feel each other's emotions telepathically. Often, I think of Kristi and at the same time get a message from her. Our Souls somehow seem to learn together, and I'm so grateful. We're Soul Sisters! We also share a belief to live the life of your Soul's highest intention or highest good. We both actively ask our Souls (higher selves) to download the information we need in order to make that happen. Being in constant gratitude, gratitude, gratitude keeps the magic flowing.

CHAPTER 17

Water Music

And I wonder if you have had the experience
Of thinking of a person
And then the phone rings
And you look at the phone
Yes, indeed
You have dialed in to
That person
An "aha" moment
A sign along the way
That we are all magically connected
A ripple effect
Of dropping a stone in the water
And watching the outward movement
A wave of understanding
A sense of meaning
An end to loneliness
That there is no separation
We have one heart
We are all the light
And like light
We are different colors
Changing moods
We are all energy
Atoms and quarks
All space
And dare I say

Some are spacier than others
Vibrating at different frequencies
And you have a chance encounter
You meet a person
You intuitively know
You are on the same wavelength
Vibrating at the same frequency
And I am reminded that
No two snowflakes are the same
Each one a slightly different shape
Just like humans
We are 90% water
And did you know that
Water crystals exposed to loving thoughts
And viewed in a microscope
Are beautifully formed
Whereas those crystals
Exposed to negative thoughts
Are malformed and fragmented
And maybe that is why
Handel composed the "Water Music"
As an apology to King George
And played it for him
On the River Thames
A return to good favor
Promoted forgiveness
A change
That was duly noted
Letting go of negativity
And what is it about the
Sound of the waves

A longing to be by the ocean
Makes me feel peaceful
A sense of tranquility
And wellbeing
And a knowing
That we are all connected
My source is the same as yours
We are both
Thinkers behind the thoughts
And the sound of the waves
Rocks me into a peaceful sleep
And I do remember that dream
Of building a home by the water
And playing Handel's "Water Music"
Releasing that intention into the Universe
Imagining it floating out of the top of my head
From my crown chakra
And the dream came true
And what will you introduce
Into that quiet space
Behind the thoughts
What Erickson called
The middle of nowhere
And Deepak Chopra calls
The state of bliss
The expanded awareness
Of being one with the Universe
What is mirrored by your intention
A quantum leap
A bird's eye holographic view
A symphony of sounds

That warm good feeling
Raising your consciousness
Day by day
Feeling better
In every way

CHAPTER 18

Pain is a Habitual Pattern

**Pain demands an audience!
Unfortunately if you are in pain
you are also the audience.**

There's a story about a retired lady in the U.K. who felt that she had too much time on her hands after her husband died. She was looking for something worthwhile to do, so she decided to raise money for charity simply by asking people to give her their loose change. Desiring to increase her return, she bought a bumble bee outfit in order to stand out more. It made people laugh, and yes, of course, people stopped and gave more. The joy that she experienced propelled her to collect money in the streets of England six days a week. She was interviewed on television once and was quoted to have said something along the lines of, "You know, on the seventh day of the week when I don't put on the bee outfit, my arthritis is killing me!"

It turns out that putting on the bee outfit was the trigger signal for joy for her body. When she was wearing it, she was inspired. I would love to have given a Drain ThatPain session to this sweet lady. However, she died last year (2017), at the ripe old age of 95. Bless her!

Randi's story

Randi Light appears in the documentary *Drain ThatPain* and also contributes a chapter on "Creating 'laser-like' thoughts that heal" in this book. I'm so grateful for Randi. We had met briefly at conventions in Las Vegas and Chicago — we only spent a few hours together. However, I instinctively knew that she needed to be an anchor in the documentary. This was not only for me, but also for our audience who I just knew would intuitively feel our connection, for our Souls recognized each other.

I knew that I needed to talk about my mother, Elizabeth Cameron, and her battle with cancer at the beginning of the documentary, and I knew I needed to do that with someone I felt really at home with. You, the audience, needed to know what inspired me to make a film about pain.

We were filmed sitting in the kitchen on stools. Our noses were four inches apart and there were three cameras on us at different angles. I looked into Randi's very safe eyes and the emotion flowed accordingly. "I'm so grateful for the time with my mother...," I spoke softly. I mist up again typing these words.

If you have a loved one who has passed to another dimension, I am sorry for your loss.

58

Your loved one's Soul, however, is always with you. I hope this book helps you to listen to your Soul and believe in messages from the unseen! It's not whether your Soul talks, but rather — have you opened up your intention and awareness to listen?

Chronic pain in Randi's body began with an acute attack (new pain or first event) in her early twenties. She was teaching a children's gymnastics class and reached into the foam pit to help a student get out. From that moment on, she was in chronic pain from head to toe for three years. She said she could not sleep on her right side, as every time she turned over the pain would begin. This is a classic example of what we call conditioned pain — a habituated pattern or program in her body.

The first event or acute attack can be quite innocuous, like simply reaching for something, or it can be something more serious, like an accident. Either way, acute pain is new pain and it needs to be checked out medically.

When Randi saw her medical doctor, she was told, "You will have to deal with this the rest of your life." Hearing those words planted a seed for the expectation of pain in Randi's body-mind! Now, of course medical doctors mean well, but they have been taught that chronic pain is structural and most of them make decisions based on that belief.

Joanna Cameron

As Drain ThatPain practitioners, we are not doctors. We do not diagnose. Our clients come to us often by referral from doctors. Most of the people I see have had chronic pain for years and are desperate to turn it off.

Since the root cause of chronic pain is actually emotional and not structural, it can be eliminated by treating it as stuck emotions or unwanted energy in the body. If you are in pain — ask yourself what message the pain is trying to convey to you. Chronic pain is like a stuck alarm — an outworn message that can become a conditioned program or habit. Again, if you have new pain, it is a message to take action or do something, get it checked out by a doctor. However, if the pain continues and does not heal in the expected time, it becomes chronic.

Randi was able to get out of chronic pain by educating herself with the understanding that the pain had already healed in her body — she could now let go of the conditioned response so that she could turn over in bed and sleep on her right side.

It is unfortunate that many people are told to not bend their bodies in a certain way or to restrict activity if they have pain. My husband used to play tennis. When he got tendonitis in his arm he was told by his doctor that giving up tennis was probably the best solution for his pain. I am one of many Drain ThatPain practitioners all over the world who will tell you that once the pain has been drained, the person can generally resume full range of motion. A word of caution though, it is best with any exercise to start slowly and listen to your body!

Chris' Story

Christopher was able to let go of knee pain during our group training and documentary filming in Nashville, but afterwards continued with physiotherapy in order to strengthen the muscles. In his case, it was best for him not to overdo things. The same applies to you, dear reader! Always be sure to listen to your intuition as you learn to reuse parts of your body that were previously restricted. Just to be clear, pain is very different than stiffness. Again, if you strengthen your intuition and really learn to listen to your body, you will understand the difference.

I once saw a client who had what is commonly known as "frozen shoulder." In our first session, she drained the pain, but needed another session to drain the stiffness. She now has full range of motion.

Believe it or not, I actually see most of my clients online and not in person, and it never fails to amaze me that healing can occur in this fashion. Facebook Messenger video works well. There are also programs like Skype or Zoom that you can use to host video chats online. I see clients all over the world using these tools.

Habitual patterns are driven by thought patterns. If you expect the pain, then your unconscious mind quite simply mirrors that intention. In my experience, fear drives more pain than any other emotion. In the documentary Cliff from Myrtle Beach says it quite clearly, "I'm not in fear anymore."

Jill's story – Installing a New Habit

I had a wonderfully validating experience at the swimming pool this morning, where l regularly swim and chat. In the locker room, Jill said to me, "Joanna, you taught me to touch myself on the forehead when I was thinking negative thoughts, and it works. I'm not in pain!" You will see me in the documentary touching people on the "third eye" or pineal gland in the forehead area. It's a positive anchor. I believe that most scientists would agree that oxytocin is released when you touch that gland. Oxytocin is the love hormone which is also secreted in much larger doses when you fall in love or orgasm, or when a woman gives birth.

Drain ThatPain enables us to let go of pain, strip away negative anchors, and install new

anchors that promote and instill loving thoughts. We are animals after all, and just like Pavlov's dogs, we know that when the school bell rings — it's time to do something.

During the war in Iraq, I had the enormous privilege to work for the U.S. Army in Germany as a comedy hypnotist. I toured the bases in Germany and performed comedy for the troops — many of whom had just come back from Iraq. I've also worked and performed for the Wounded Warriors Regiment, who hold "The Marine Corps Trials" which feature paralympic sports including: wheelchair basketball, sitting volleyball, swimming, recumbent cycling, shooting, archery at Camp Pendleton in San Diego every year. It's amazing to watch these men play basketball in wheelchairs. It's wildly competitive!

In conversations I've had with soldiers and marines, we've chatted about Phantom Limb Pain. Phantom Limb Pain can be experienced when a soldier loses an arm or leg and the pain in the affected organ remains, even though there is no limb! This is similar to the experience a person has when they complain of tooth pain after they've had the tooth extracted, and there's no longer a nerve there to feel pain!

Chronic pain, which can be experienced in a nerve, muscle, or tendon is a message, or rather a program in the brain that is outdated. It can be let go!

CHAPTER 19

Rhona-Bee
Rhona Wands

I met Joanna in a Facebook group, discussing pain elimination, and I decided to reach out and ask for help with chronic back, neck and shoulder pain. She replied to my comment immediately, offering to help me there and then.

Straight away our energetic-telepathic connection was magnetically clear. The process of removing my (correction – That) longterm pain had already begun. I was ready to disown in, put it outside my body. And yes — at the right place, at the right time, with the right person. Of course, it is ALWAYS the right person.

Joanna invited me to go Facebook live to remove that pain, and so this is what we did. We connected via live video and neither of us could have known what was about to take place. I am based in Scotland, and Joanna in America. This proves to me that distance can never separate our connection to one another.

**I have long been known as Rhona-Bee.
The Bee is my power animal and holds many
meanings for my journey in life.**

Well — right in the middle of our live video, when Joanna and I had our eyes closed and were connecting to remove chronic pain (the origin of which I can no longer even tell you) — a giant Queen Bumble Bee landed right on Joanna's third eye, or pineal gland! I can still actually almost taste this sweetness like the Bee's nectar, filling my body with beautiful golden honey, and taking with it, anything not aligned with my purpose — the intention of being pain free.

Having had such a spiritually strong connection from the moment we met and believing whole heartedly in the magic that WOULD be taking place,

I knew something magical and confirmative was going to happen!

My Rhona-Bee came to Joanna to channel the necessary healing for me to begin to start moving that blocked energy in my body.

And what has happened since? It is undeniable that this event set me on a journey of self discovery and opening of my heart center, and that is exactly what I have done. Pain free of course...it was gone! Not only was it gone, I was, and still am opening up to my most authentic self. Now I know how to get energy blockages (pain) moving freely again in my body. My life has shifted to such a positive state of clarity, authenticity and alignment – not without some wobbles, but I am fully able to take responsibility for my creative reality. Now, that's something I used to feel held me back, as I was too busy carrying everyone else's load.

Now I am light, free, flying like Rhona-Bee, exactly who I am supposed to be.

I do believe one has to experience Joanna's unique, loving and intentional energy to truly understand that pain CAN be removed — forever. I know I have this gift now also, and much, much more. Allowing myself to just BE (aha) — accepting my right to be here walking on this earth. And without me, you, us, the world would be a little less whole.

My message to you, dear reader! Just allow yourself to be unapologetically whole, right now. If you are in pain, imagine it being like a road block, and your physical body is the car. We want you to step into your higher energetic body and remove that road block from a higher perspective. And like breathing a sigh of relief, just allow your body to settle back into itself — allowing your physical body to move freely and easily again, filling yourself up with something wonderful. It can be a golden light, a sweet nectar, even a pizza mmm mmm — knowing you can do this process again if you ever need too.

Another piece of guidance I would offer anyone in any kind of pain — find laughter again! Much of that pain I realized was because I had not laughed in so long. The more I laugh in life, the more flexible my spine, neck and body become and the more open I am to the ease of ever-flowing abundance in my life. Focus on laughter! And how good, light and funny it feels to laugh. It works every time. Never take yourself or life too seriously.

To a truly special lady, with a uniquely divine purpose; Joanna — not only does she bring heaven to earth, but facilitating in her Midas touch helped me to bring God within. Look carefully and you'll see me in the trees at 1300.

CHAPTER 20

Dr. John Sarno

Randi talks in the documentary about how reading Dr. John Sarno's books helped her to understand that her body was conditioned to the pain and that through reading them she was able to let go of the last "little bits." Truth disbands pain in the subconscious mind.

Dr. John Sarno (1923-2017), a surgeon working at the Rusk Institute in New York in 1991, wrote *Healing Back Pain: The Mind-Body Connection,* his first of six books, all on the subject of pain. His work is the backbone of Drain ThatPain. His shoulders are the foundations on which we stand as Drain ThatPain practitioners. His work is truly inspirational. Just one example is the fact that he noticed that the structural issues in his patients' X-rays (Magnetic Resonance Imaging had not been invented then) did not necessarily match their experiences of pain. A person with "crumbling spine" (now there's a dreadful name) might not have had any pain, whereas a person with one bulging disc may have been in agony. It made no sense to him, as he noted, that a bulging disc is not necessarily painful. So then what was causing the pain?

Tension myositis syndrome "TMS" was the term Dr. Sarno coined for a lack of oxygen to

musculature at the site of the pain in the acute attack. This causes inflammation, heat, swelling, redness, and pain. The good news is that these issues heal very quickly and do no lasting damage to the tissue.

If pain continued, he determined it was emotionally based, perpetuated by expectation. It literally became a habitual negative pattern. Now, the bee suit (remember the bee lady) is the reverse. The suit served as an anchor for a positive pattern of joy and happiness. So it is possible to replace old patterns with new! I'm not suggesting that we all wear bee suits, however!

Thousands of people have let go of pain simply reading Dr. Sarno's books. People resonate with the emotional underpinnings of chronic pain, the power of expectation, and the story lines. Dr. Sarno's theories give people hope and new thought patterns, and that's where the magic can and does happen — because people don't get out of pain by being despondent, you know!

In spite of Sarno's well-documented research and his six books, the concept of chronic pain being emotional and treated as such is not yet a consistent thought in the American psyche. If you watch the "evening news" in the United States, every other advertisement is about a drug for chronic pain. The culture in the U.S.A. is that of looking for the "quick fix," and the advertisements condition people to believe that drugs can ameliorate, solve the pain, or even prevent "irreversible" bone loss. Hear me now — your body can make new bone. That's what happens when you fracture a limb, for instance. You are given a cast to immobilize the limb so that the bones "knit together again" as your body makes new bone!

So if the answer is to educate and inspire people about pain elimination, then the question for me became, "How could I reach more people in a different way?" One of the answers I discovered was that I could make a documentary with a creative team, and present truthful story lines of people in pain in order to educate, inspire, and assist others in imagining a world without chronic pain.

Just as people let go of by pain reading books, they can also leave it behind in their movie seats. Education, inspiration and imagination are the keys to letting go, and loving intention is paramount!

The word "psychosomatic" (meaning mind/body) used to be in favor as a way to describe physical conditions which were considered to be influenced by the mind. One example would be irritable bowel syndrome (IBS). IBS appears as an overly sensitive digestive system with bouts of both constipation and diarrhea. The digestive system is controlled by your unconscious mind, which digests your food and then gives you a conscious message when it's time to eliminate that which is not needed — and go to the bathroom. Second only to the heart, more information goes from your digestive system to the brain than from any other organ. The stomach is energetically linked to your personal power, which is diminished by anxiety and fear. You can let go of these negative emotions using Drain ThatPain.

The term psychosomatic may not be in fashion anymore, however, its meaning remains part of our language. We've all heard the term "nervous stomach." I remember a time in the 1980's when gastric ulcers were thought to be caused by stress — conversely, gastric ulcers became "fashionable" at that time.

When people were overly stressed, they believed that they might get an ulcer, so many actually did. Today, IBS or similar autoimmune disorders such as fibromyalgia, lupus, and arthritis are more in vogue.

Raye's story

Raye had lupus until August of 2017, and her story is featured in the documentary, *Drain ThatPain*. Since draining her pain, she has been free of lupus, and her health and energy have returned. She now has the ability to move forward with big goals. Raye's feature in the movie was filmed in Savannah where she works as a clinical hypnotherapist. Further adding to the synchronicities of life, I happened to meet Raye at the same conference where I met Kristi, who as you will recall, let go of grief in the same session.

Another example of a mind-body syndrome is carpal tunnel, which affects the hands. When it first became a widely spread diagnosis, it was thought to be a response to overuse of the hands while typing, exacerbated by the multiplicity of the personal computer in the 1980's (creating a new hand-work syndrome)! However, people typed on old typewriters for years that were much harder on the hands than the new computer keyboards, and for some reason they never got these conditions. The well meaning medical profession has preferred to give names and make nouns in order to describe body processes. So carpal tunnel syndrome became a new thing, and people attached their own beliefs and expectations to it.

Chris' story

While filming the *Drain ThatPain* documentary, I met Chris on a bridge in Nashville and found out that she had thumb pain. This made it difficult for her to open jam jars, hold onto to her glasses, etc. She believed that the origin of her pain was structural, caused by carrying very large text books as a math teacher for 35 years. However, when she got to the emotional meaning of that pain, she understood that what she really wanted was to be doing something else with her life. Her body-mind was giving her a message.

Pain is a message. The challenge is to inhabit it, listen to it, and change accordingly by creating new habits that encourage positive thoughts and feelings of wellbeing.

The Drain ThatPain methodology allows you to drain away old conditioning and undesirable habits. When you purge the unwanted energy of chronic pain, your own energy surges. You thrive, and your imagination opens up as you get on with your fabulous life. Start by imagining that now, why don't you? Feel how the energy begins to increase in your body.

CHAPTER 21

Nest Eggs

Now as you are sitting there
Imagining my words
I want to say how sorry I am
For that pain
But rest assured that we take this journey together
And you can give yourself the present
Of understanding that discomfort
Is a message about connectivity
For you, your mind, body and Soul
And possibly your relationships
So you can relax with your mind open
In a mindful state
Just as I become transfixed on the golf course
As I look into a pond,
With my golf ball retriever in hand
I see all kinds of pond life
Tadpoles in different stages of growth
Some bigger, some smaller
Will I see a white flash of a golf ball
That draws me in or is it just a rock
And the excitement of reaching
one that seems too far out
Bringing it to the surface
Buried treasure of great value
A diamond in the rough

And the joy of its discovery
Wiping off the mud
And bringing it back to life
And I remember a time many years ago
When my sister and I would go
To the neighbor's egg farm
Little girls in search of magical freshly laid eggs
And the warm smell of the hay barn
Where we wanted to jump and play hide and seek
But the farmer's instructions were to collect the eggs
And place them carefully in our baskets
And the anticipation of our search
Would there be one, two, or three freshly laid eggs
Where yesterday, there were none
Warm with straw attached
Lying next to a white china egg
Upon which a broody hen sits and clucks and in turn
Motivates and stimulates the whole process
Just as I am motivated to assist you
To learn what you need to learn
Because you too can fly again
Out of the mud
On the fairway of life
Because it all belongs to you

CHAPTER 22

Pain as a Distraction

"It has been said that physical pain is the brain's way of protecting the individual from the emotional pain they are afraid to experience. Realizing that can promote immediate progress in many cases."
– Amanda Wright

Drain ThatPain is simple — educate, inspire, and imagine. Chronic pain is emotional — Let it go! That's what your Soul wants!

The first line of the *Drain ThatPain* trailer is, "Pain changes people."

Pain wears you down with anxiety and slows you down physically so much that you may stop moving. Pain is a message, and chronic pain is a stuck alarm that may sound louder if it's not attended to. Movement and general wellbeing go hand-in-hand, so I like to perform the Drain ThatPain method with you standing up:

1) Standing up creates an atmosphere of movement and change. Your body is saying, "OK, what's next?" It's a positive expectation of mov-

ing out of pain and leaving it behind — A wanted distraction!

2) I can understand your energy better when my body faces yours. My chakras and heart energy are closer-aligned with you this way.

3) I can also intuit pain by looking at how you hold your body. Pain broadcasts its own signal. For example, you may be slumped in the shoulders with your head protruding forward. How you feel is manifested in your body posture. The most important factor of how you are perceived and how you perceive yourself is posture. I work a great deal with all my clients on this issue.

4) Once the pain has drained, you can literally step out of it — a powerful metaphor that it's over. It becomes clear that this is pain elimination, not pain management.

From Posture to Power Exercise

Give it a go right now! Stand up and relax your shoulders and align your head with your spine. How does that feel? When I do that, my stomach feels happier. Remember your chakras? Well, the stomach is where your solar plexus is — it's the root of your power! If you've ever noticed how models walk, their stomachs protrude. It's OK! You can do that too! When you feel powerful, it manifests in your posture. Buddha has a large stomach and uses it.

In the last ten minutes of the documentary, I sit in

a chair and literally *Drain ThatPain* with you, the audience. I had a cushion behind the base of my spine for comfort. When I looked back at the film I said, "Oh my — I have a Buddha stomach!" Since then it's always been known as the Buddha scene — a compliment! Good posture begins with your body, which mirrors your intention — so make it a habit! Taking care to stand or sit with good posture not only helps your body look better, but it also works energetically and gives you energy.

Chronic pain is a message that you need to move as much and as often as you are able. Our bodies are supposed to move, but oftentimes people restrict their movement. Their energy, stress level, posture, and general wellness suffer.

Jane's Story

Jane's presenting problem was fibromyalgia. As a driven, self-described perfectionist who worked in the stock market, she would often soothe her nervous clients by ratcheting up her work schedule. During the stock market collapse in 2007, she admittedly worked many more hours than were healthy for her overall wellbeing.

And then her body quite literally laid her in

her bed. She said everything hurt! She had brain fog and migrating pain — sometimes her feet hurt so badly that she could not put her shoes on. No longer able to work, she had been on disability since that time.

I performed three Drain ThatPain sessions on Jane over a three month period, and gradually she learned to turn the pain down to a level that was comfortable for her.

Your body has the choice in a *Drain ThatPain* session. You can rest assured that your body-mind is never going to leave you unprotected, as that is its chief objective. It will only turn the pain down to the level that is desirable at that time.

Jane's body (her "meat suit") dutifully protected her at the onset of danger. Her stress level was so high that her body said, "Enough already — draw the curtains!" Once Jane drained that pain, she was able to put her shoes on, go for a walk, and start moving more and more as she felt better. The brain fog lifted, and positive thoughts predominated — she had turned the tide around.

As time went on, Jane began to understand that the origin of her pain ran deeper than just overworking her mind and body in her job. She realized that she had put too much pressure on herself to be perfect. She wanted to be happy

more than she wanted to be right, so she would catch herself if she found herself trying to manipulate or control others. What she learned is that she could let go of the need to judge others and herself — the "Judge" within. This realization proved to be very important.

As Jane continued her healing journey, she felt the importance of establishing a safe space to tune in to her mind, body, and spirit. She chose to do this through spiritual reading, meditation, and listening to audio books as she went walking and literally got back on her feet again. As she honored herself by putting time aside daily for herself, she got better. Although Jane still feels stress, she said that the knowledge that she has a safe space of meditation she can return to carries her through. She had to unlearn to inhabit stress and pain — that's why education is so important.

Pain is the ultimate "make it go away" distraction. It closes down the senses as creativity disappears, and the curtains close as a person in chronic pain withdraws from social life. Relationships suffer, and marriages fall apart. Pain robs people of joy in their lives. And because a person in pain does not move as much, the body further suffers.

"Pain can only feed on pain. Pain cannot feed on joy. It finds it quite indigestible"
- Eckhart Tolle

Chronic pain does not mean that there's something

inherently wrong with you, or that you are less than magnificent, frail, or not able to live and move happily as you engage in life on earth. Instead, remember to think of pain as an alarm in your body — a warning system.

Pain is the protective response of the body. It alerts you that something is awry — danger is afoot! It's also important to remember that new pain, the first acute attack or seemingly innocuous event, is a message to take action. Chronic pain means that you may have healed physically, but there is something emotional that you still need to learn.

Dr. John Sarno's work has helped us to understand that the body creates pain as a distraction, because there is something that the person does not want to look at. It's a smokescreen! Just as a magician does a sleight of hand and distracts you when they are really reaching for a dove in the hat!

Your body wants to protect you from the negative emotions of the primitive mind — rage and fear. In many ways, your body-mind is a child.

Have you ever watched children hearing or seeing something that they do not like and intuitively covering their ears or their eyes? Your body-mind does the same thing — it's a "make it go away" gesture!

Animals have a way of just "shaking off" fear. My

husband and I have cats that live both inside and out-side. During baby chipmunk season, I am often pre-sented with what looks like a dead chipmunk. The poor thing is totally loose and limp in my cat's mouth. I talk to the cat (and cats do talk if you train them), who responds by dropping the chipmunk. I then put a flower pot upside down over the chipmunk so the an-imal has air and light. The cats disappear from the scene, and when I return the chipmunk is invariably alive and ready to run away. It literally has "shaken it off," and presumably forgotten it.

Humans, with our large cerebral lobes have the ability and the tendency to ruminate on events and bottle-up negative emotions. Drain ThatPain is a "shake-off" of negative emotions. Once they are gone, you no longer feel them. Instead you come alive and thrive!

CHAPTER 23

Perfectionism and Good-ism

One of Dr. Sarno's many discoveries was that there are certain personality behaviors that are found in people with chronic pain. The first of these behaviors is using perfectionism as a measure of success. I would suggest to anyone in chronic pain that letting go of negative judgment of yourself and others is very important. Just let it go and let it be. When you judge yourself negatively, you are literally beating yourself up and the pain is worse as the Soul is saying, "No, no — listen to me!" Judging others also really does leave a bad taste in the mouth. Understand that you cannot and you do not need to control everything around you — and what a relief! Your job is to dream and live a life that complements your passions and talents. So put one foot in front of the other and trust in the Universe and your intuition to guide you. Relax into your life and focus on the moment at hand.

Attend to the present — intend for the future.

The next personality trait Dr. Sarno often found in people with chronic pain was "good-ism." At the base of good-ism is guilt and the inability to forgive yourself. These well meaning people want to smooth over situations and will forgive others easily, but they have lost contact with their own Soul. They need to learn to forgive themselves. Good-ism is often found in highly empathic people who have issues with boundaries. They take on other peoples pain as their own. Some Good-ists actually believe that worrying about a situation helps.

If you see yourself in the above descriptions, that's a good thing because it means that you are on the way to putting pain behind you. I've watched my clients let go of pain when I simply tell them about the above behavioral characteristics. A light switch of understanding occurs. Understanding the problem is often enough to simply let pain go in conversation. Quite simply, I can often "talk" people out of pain. Remaining in gratitude and continual self-monitoring of your own behavior so that the "judge" and the "victim" do not appear in your thoughts and your speech is sometimes all that's required to drain pain away.

The Universe probably understands sarcasm if the intention is a bit of comedy, but blame doesn't get you anywhere except more of the same. That's right — the Universe is a reflector and it feeds it all right back to you! Everybody is responsible for their own feelings.

CHAPTER 24

Hopscotch

Maybe you remember playing hopscotch
Giggling with a school friend
Finding the chalk and
Drawing the lines on the pavement
Throwing a stone
Onto the correct square
And then retrieving it
Careful not to tread on those lines
Or you lose your turn
Carefully balancing on one foot
As you turn and face another direction
And the rules are borders
Lines in the sand
Necessary boundaries
To play the game
And what did Robert Frost say
Fences make good neighbors
Now we see white flags in people's gardens
That post the same message
A so-called invisible fence
So that their dog stays in their yard
And remains safe
Happy in the knowledge
That it is protecting their property
But in some cultures

The rules are different
The Germans for instance
Do not use fences
They place a seat in their garden
To allow access to a hiker
Who can wander in
Of her own free will
And relax for a while
Totally safe
In their garden
And there are boundaries that limit us
I am reminded of Roger Bannister
Who was told that
The four minute mile would never be broken
He accepted the challenge
He refused to be fenced in
By that thought
And ran a mile in less than 240 seconds
Nothing is impossible, he said
All it takes is imagination
And so I wonder
What will happen
As you imagine
Your opportunities for the future
What imagined boundaries will you leap over
As you focus on the dream
The end result
And act as if
It's already happening
Because your unconscious mind
Loves intention

The rudder on the boat
Gives it direction
And all you have to do
Is focus on the moment
With the end result in mind
Attend to the present
Enjoy the ride
As you intend for the future

CHAPTER 25

The Placebo Effect

The Placebo effect is when someone takes a medication or has a chronic pain surgery, believing that it will have a positive effect. And it does! Why does that happen? Because the person has set intention. In this case self-loving intention which is the strongest force in the Universe.

Intention combined with action produces manifestation!

Dr. John Sarno suggested in his writings that in the case of successful surgery for chronic pain, it is the placebo effect that the patient experiences. However, he wrote there is a "symptom imperative," so if the emotional cause of the chronic pain is not addressed, then the chronic pain moves somewhere else. Sadly, I see well intentioned doctors chasing pain with surgeries. Because that is what they have been taught to do.

Later in the book you will read Cliff's story of letting go of pain, and, the efforts his loving-wife, Billie, made to assist him, even using the placebo effect to his advantage. I quote from her Facebook post.

"Cliff was on a pain-med that looked just like a little saccharin pill, so I replaced them to keep him from getting addicted with an over-the-counter sleeping pill. I would buy that pill and lick the label off the side of every gelcap and put them in his sleeping pill bottle. He slept just as well and never got a headache."

May I take this opportunity to say how moved I am by caregivers like Billie who go the extra mile to help their loved ones! My heart and thanks go out to you all.

CHAPTER 26

Water Heals

**"Water has a message for the world. The world
is linked together by love and gratitude.
The message of water is Love and Gratitude"
— Masaru Emoto**

I've always been fascinated by water. I grew up
within walking distance of the River Itchen in Shawford, Hampshire, England. The chalk-based, spectac-
ularly clear stream was my playground as a child. In
those days we were free to roam as children, and we
played all day on and by the river.

**Watching the bright green river weed
majestically swaying beneath the stream
surface, I suddenly saw a brook trout appear —
yet it was always there, totally camouflaged
and seeming translucent. It was just biding its
time, treading water against the current as a
dragonfly landed on an impossibly white water
lily. I wondered to myself — "How could a
moment be any more beautiful?"**

I'm totally entranced by beautiful clear rivers and
streams and have fond memories of when my father
and I would go dry fly fishing! The goal of dry fly fishing is to float your fly on the mirror-like water with a

special floating fishing line. When we wandered by the stream to look for fish, we would watch the water as a fish rose or sometimes leaped above the surface with a "plop!" "Which fly was it eating?" I wondered. "Can I put my fly right on the surface, so it floats above the fish?" The peaceful contemplation was total absorption for me, even when I inevitably caught the fishing line on a tree whilst casting the fly.

The ocean has a similar pull for me and "Oh, my, do I love the sound!" I am spiritually renewed by water in all its iterations, including steam rooms, champagne bubbles, misty English days, and skiing through light fresh powder snow in the Utah mountains. The latter is a thrill all of its own! Of course I can't leave out the Splash Girls, our ad hoc women's swimming group at a local high school pool where I swim most mornings, and the joy, laughter, and yes — the journey that brings.

Our bodies are water. We are watery souls and live on this "blue planet" because of water! Even though to our primitive sense organs it appears that we live solely in solid form, everything in fact has a vibration and a resonance. We are actually all energy at our core, and we give off massive vibrations to the world. Whether you believe in energy or not, it's all about trusting the unseen.

You may not be able to see this energy, but you can

certainly feel it. Maybe you have had the feeling of watching the energy change when a person walks into the room, or that feeling of resonance when you've met a like-minded Soul. You may find yourself smiling in recognition at the thought.

Your "vibe" is the intention of your thoughts and feelings. Love is the highest vibration. Being in love is awesome whether it's with a person or whether it's being aligned with your purpose — your Soul's highest intention for your life on this planet. When you are fully connected and integrated with your mind, body, and Soul, you align yourself with creation — manifestation is your middle name!

Animals have their own vibrations as well. Our marmalade cat, Wallie, crouched and held onto the floor at least thirty seconds before I felt the earth shake in the 5.4 Virginia Earthquake a couple of years ago. There are also lovely stories of empathetic elephants picking up frightened people as the elephants intuitively knew it was time to head for higher ground when a tsunami approached.

You can bet our ancestors had a much clearer idea of the weather picture than we do. They could feel it on their skin, smell the approaching air, and hear the expectant sounds, as all their senses tuned in when the weather was changing and a Nor'easter was approaching. They understood life in a different way then. Even though we haven't yet been able to comprehend it, maybe we can relearn.

Cloud-busting exercise
(Thank You Maseru Emoto!)

You are much more powerful than you think you are. Water simply absorbs our vibe, which is made up of our intentions and our feelings. Clouds are evaporated water — essentially steam. You can intend for them to disappear using your energy. The perfect day for this is a puffy-cloud day with a brilliant blue sky. I do this standing in a powerful stance, with my shoulders relaxed.

1) Get into a powerful stance outside. Feel the power in your stomach.

2) Close your eyes. Align the power in your stomach with your intuition chakra in the middle of your forehead. Open up your divine chakra which spins white at the top of your head. Watch as the color yellow morphs to a light blue and white.

3) Open your eyes. Pick a cloud in the sky. Study its shape.

4) Close your eyes. Imagine that shape disappearing. Outstretch your arm with splayed fingers and say out loud, "The cloud is disappearing."

5) Bring all your energy to the cloud with your eyes closed.

6) See it disappear in your mind's eye. Say out loud, "Thank you!"

7) Open your eyes.

8) It can take a few minutes but that cloud will break up and disappear.

Once you have done that with a smaller cloud, move on to a bigger cloud. If you do this with a like-minded friend, you'll find that your energy is at least twice as powerful. So now that you've moved steam, you can certainly move water.

Look upon water as your extended self. Since you are mostly water, it's just you in another form. Water is the ultimate chameleon, it can form ice and then actually float within itself!

You can only see that in life which is inside of you. You are both the observer and the observed. Your energy vibration into the world is your reflection — it's you as an energetic being. You can only change your life by going inside! Since you get in life what you intend — we can collectively change the earth by raising our individual vibrations and intending for a world that lives harmoniously and peacefully and has drained away negative emotions.

We must always learn from nature. Abundance is everywhere! The Laws of Nature are clear. There are no negative emotions and nature lives in harmony. Just as we had the power to create negative emotions to protect our fragile ego minds that were grappling with fear — we also have the power as empathetic humans to

bring heaven to Earth using our collective loving intention, imagination, and combined vibration.

There is no clearer example that negative emotions are man made than to look at water crystals. I am so thankful to Masaru Emoto for his love of water crystals and subsequent research, that proved that water reacts to emotions. Emoto showed us that water forms crystals at a certain temperature, and when you look at them with a microscope and a light you can see different forms due to the emotions in the water. In his studies, Emoto was able to prove that love and gratitude produce beautiful, well-formed crystals that can multiply; and human emotions of anger, sadness, guilt, and shame produce malformed crystals that are unstable and energetically stagnant.

So here it is then — nature does not do negative emotions. Humans do, but we don't need to. Nature, in response to negative emotions, creates malformed crystals that are lifeless, stagnant, and devoid of energy. Nature flows and knows only perfection, and we are privileged to see this divinity in the fleeting presence of loving and grateful water crystals. Nature is positive loving energy that expands both outwardly and inwardly.

Nature is energy, radiance, and life force. It's crystalline love, a frozen love song, architecture in motion, and enthusiasm! To be inspired is to be continually filled with that love song and to feel that sense of one-ness in your body.

Inspiration is allowing your mind to travel through rainbows of light as your chakras are aligned — spinning magically with the color of rainbows and opening up the magical corridor of your body-mind to the higher self — your divinity and your Soul.

As I write this Aretha Franklin, "The Sound of Soul," is being remembered. We all know how our Souls react to music, but how does water react to sound, or to a written vibration? Ever curious, Masaru Emoto set up a container of water with the word "Love" written on it and then examined the crystals. The water formed the same beautifully formed crystals as water exposed to loving thoughts. How does this happen? Can the water read? In a way — yes! Whether the loving vibration came from the words themselves or the person who wrote those words, the water formed the same loving crystals. The words "Love" and "Gratitude" produced the most wonderful crystals, and the same crystals also appeared when the water was exposed to love songs.

Coincidences, in my world and yours too, are gifts from the Universe that let you know that you are on your path. When I looked at Masaru Emoto's pictures, I noticed that he had a picture of the beautiful crystal that water formed when exposed to Bach's "Arioso in G," also called "Air on a G." That was the same composition that was playing in the Willard Hotel when I had a spiritual knowing, with every molecule of my being, that my mother's Soul-presence was right there in that room! When I saw Emoto's water crystal picture I was awestruck, and had goosebumps tingling through my spine and fingers. Masaru Emoto's book, *The Hidden Messages in Water*, has sat on my bookshelf for at least ten years. However, I never saw that wondrous crystal and made the connection. I have opened up my intuition, and I now see these amazing signs — in all their majesty.

Inspired by this discovery, I have started a spiritual meditation group. We meditate for four minutes a day at 0900 EST, U.S.A. Join us as we visualize a huge sign over Niagara Falls with the words LOVE and GRATITUDE, and then see the water flowing that loving energy into the groundwater and then into the atmosphere to give us steam and rain.

We visualize ourselves drinking the water, bathing in the water, and celebrating the feeling of a walk in the fresh smell of a misty English morning with the sun breaking through. All the while, we are holding the loving intention and gratitude for water in all its iterations as it brings Heaven to Earth. As you visualize with us, perhaps there's a wave you want to bathe in, maybe the ocean itself. Maybe you can even hear it?

**Thank you, thank you, Blue Planet
for the gift of water — life itself**

CHAPTER 27

Intention and Inspiration

The *Drain ThatPain* documentary is about pain elimination. Unabashedly, it's an experiential, "Heal The World Movie," produced with the intention that audience members can let go of chronic pain in their movie seats and leave it behind! Spiritually, we can move intention on our planet so we can rise above fear and chronic pain. Love rules over pain. *Drain That-Pain* shows how education, inspiration, and imagination can move the stuck energy of chronic pain safely and globally.

There are lots of "I" words there — Intention, Inspiration and Imagination — III — that looks a bit like numerology, doesn't it? One, one, one — 111. I find joy in that! Recognition — the Universe knows that I love 111, and it keeps giving it to me in so many ways. Our crew began the group filming on November 11, 2017, then this happened...

Darren Williams, the director of the *Drain That-Pain* documentary, had a very large, heavy book (The Pain Book). The idea was that Randi Light and I would throw the book together with the comment, "There is so much written about pain, but really all we know is that if you dropped the book, it might hurt your foot!" When I looked back at the footage, I noticed that Randi and I threw that book at 11:11am on the morning of the filming! I assure you that was not written into any script. Actually, there wasn't even a script until later in the movie, but even then, no one on screen was scripted! It all happened intuitively as the Universe provided direction.

So if you, dear reader or listener, start seeing the 111 — thank the Universe and ask it to give you more of the same. It will respond and you will find inspiration that comes with it, and it multiplies all on its own. Begin to see the Universe as your reflection — your friend! Slow down, relax into the moment, and you will expand your consciousness! You will find that time expands and you can accomplish more and feel grounded and content in the moment.

Joy in life comes from extraordinary places and spaces, but real, inspirational, spine-tingling, buzz-filled moments are remembered! It's a feeling of immense grace and peacefulness when "time stands still!" This is actually quite true — as it's one moment in time. One of my greatest "frozen in time" moments was experiencing Chelsea's birth and the pure miracle of holding her for the first time.

My mother's Soul appearance shook me in the Willard Hotel. I knew in that moment that we are all "Souls," who can be here or there in any moment; that time is only an earthly measurement of space, but most of all — that our Souls remain.

Delving into these concepts, you can begin to build

trust in what I call the "unseen!" Just because you can't see it doesn't mean that there isn't a great deal happening in the unseen to allow your dreams to come true. Just learn to trust, and open up your awareness!

There is an infinite intelligence and we are all one with that collective unconscious — our shared source. We have all always belonged. It's just taken us some time, or perhaps many lifetimes, to comprehend that earthly beings have a tendency to believe our "always right ego-minds" that measure us in some inauthentic, Soul-blinded, earthly way. How silly is this when the truth is that we are spiritual beings — made of love, and living in self-chosen journeys on this planet, so that we might learn that we are actually gods that can align with the Universe to create anything that we want — including bringing Heaven to Earth!

The Universe works like a navigational device. When you get into your vehicle, you put your safety belt on first, then switch on your car, and then set the navigation by adding the address. Your navigation system, GPS or NAV, focuses like the Universe does on your intention — on the end result, and it will faithfully take you there. You only have to surrender to that and trust it — you don't need to know how. You don't have to worry about the details. That's the detachment that is needed. You have already delegated the process, so now you can just think about your driving or whatever you create with your mind on the open road. You don't have to think about how the car works or look under the hood/bonnet — you just take the necessary steps and detach from the process.

Your intention then is the end result. It's the rudder on the dinghy that gives it direction. What is it that you want? Make a picture of that and incorporate the feelings into it. What are you hearing? Applause maybe? Your own applause — your self-love — and most of all your feelings! Let it be about love.

It's best to make big goals that come from your values. Most importantly the goals must be about you, so focus on self-love, the feeling of you being truly content in your own skin.

Money will flow alongside love — as money goes where energy flows. Remember that the Laws of Nature and Emoto's research tell us that negative emotions produce stagnant, malformed crystals — so let's choose loving intention instead, creating nature's perfection with beautiful crystals and abundance everywhere.

Always pick the highest intention. If money is your intention, what's the higher goal? Who will benefit from that money? What increased loving energy will that money bring to you, your family, and our planet Earth?

Remember, the Universe absolutely obeys your intentions, and of course our intentions are like us — primarily unconscious. So if you believe that money doesn't grow on trees and that it's hard to come by, that will be your reality — poverty consciousness.

Joanna Cameron

It's best to give the Universe goals like more happiness, success, and laughter with friends. When you have that, the money flows! Yes, link your goals to happiness and money, but let happiness, love and gratitude seep through your body. See those words in the water of your body and feel them cleanse every nerve, cell, fiber of your body, washing away any negative energy and leaving you energized.

I've followed the feeling of watching people let go of pain. Nothing ever has inspired me more than that feeling. It gives me purpose! I am here on this planet as a messenger to teach people and train practitioners to honor their Souls as they move towards self-love, and to let go of pain as they integrate body, mind, and Soul together to reach their Souls' highest intention.

Intention and inspiration are your vibration. Let's make that loving intention. The closer you move towards love, the higher your vibration. What we really do as Drain ThatPain practitioners (and our numbers are growing worldwide) is move people closer to love — and self-love comes first!

There is a difference between ego-love and self-love... I'm going to let those words hang till the next chapter. For some reason, as I was typing this I stopped in mid sentence. Then, I looked back at the word count, it was 11,111 words at 11:11am. It seems there was a tectonic shift in the earth!

What am I doing? I continually imagine and dream. I'm acting as if the Universe has already shifted as millions of people get out of chronic pain, reading this book, and watching the documentary. Now, that's what I call bringing heaven to earth!

CHAPTER 28

Ego-love and Self-love

It's a strange phenomenon that if you ask people what they want for themselves, they may mention various things, including more stuff or more abundance. But if you ask those same people what they want for their loved ones, they will use terms such as peacefulness, happiness, and being in love. Therein lies the paradox.

When you are born onto this Earth, you have convenient amnesia to the fact that you are an infinite being and your Soul can ascend to higher dimensions. As a baby you are born into a spiritual world as a universal being. In your new "meat suit," you arrive with survival love and, of course survival instincts. In your new physical body you are given opposable thumbs and the ability to clasp. As a baby, you are in the spiritual-exploratory-bliss of the moment as you gurgle and live in suspended time — your wants fulfilled with your built-in alarm system that keeps your parents informed of your needs. Soon you learn to stand, walk, and ponder the meaning of the word "mine" for what seems like eternity during your second year (your 2's).

As a two-year old, you are testing boundaries and pondering what is "mine" and what is "not-mine," as well as what belongs and what doesn't. Also fascinating is how malleable your beliefs can be as a child.

Our Buddha baby knows that she can swim, as she's been in the womb. She is then rightfully told as soon as she can walk not to play close to pools, as she could fall in. The child is given the message — "You can't swim." Later our child is given swimming lessons so she can remember how to swim again. A child's beliefs may change up to three times about swimming in the early years.

Children take things very personally and then can make wrong assumptions about their worth, as if the child could be anything less than magnificent, and a blessing.

When they learn ego-love from a young age, children can quickly define themselves by the quality or lack of toys, their abilities in sports, or how they measure up against others. It is the self-berating, demeaning lies that children tell themselves about their own self worth that are damaging. Parental lack of involvement, bullying, sexual abuse, poverty, and verbal and non-verbal abuse can all contribute to negative conditioning in the early years. It is this footprint — the negative conditioning, shame, anger, and fear from childhood that become the negative conditioning that can lead to chronic pain. The conscious mind is thought to really begin development around the age of seven years. Ego-love is about the self wanting gratification, recognition, and respect for accomplishments. Ego-love can be frugal when it comes to others, but often extravagant when it comes to self.

Ego-love is judgmental, frequently manipulative, and competitive, as other people are judged "winners and losers." Self-love on the other hand is neither judgmental of others nor affected by their judgment. It is gracious, exhibits random acts of kindness, and is reflective by nature as it sees beauty in all things and people.

Self-love is ever-expanding energetically, enthusiastically passionate. It is a magnet for other high vibrational Souls. People with high vibrations are intention personified. They are passionate about what they do and are usually givers — philanthropists following compassionate dreams with a global agenda as a force for good. Healers are often found in this high vibe group, and these kind Souls bring Heaven to Earth. High vibe dreamers focus on big dreams and act as if their dreams are already coming true in their lives. They are not consumed with what other people think of them. They are optimistically cheerful, radiant, and passionate about what they do, as they attract people, events, and circumstances into their lives which become the catalysts of their dreams come true.

I've always loved the stage. As children, my sister and I had a small puppet theatre made by a carpenter in the shipyard where my father was both engineer and manager. Our mother sewed the red velvet curtain that we were very proud of! I started on stage in childhood in our local village Christmas pantomime and loved it! As an entertainer, I've consistently put myself in front of larger audiences, as I always wanted to be on the big stage. Imagine my thrill when I made it onto *Britain's Got Talent* as a comedy hypnotist! I made a magnificent entrance from the back of the awe-inspiring Dominion Theater in London. But after that, things did not go quite as planned, and all I can remember was the deafening sound of four buzzers going off. I don't even remember what the judges said — I was in shock! That's a blessing right there!

As I walked off Dominion Stage feeling pretty devastated, knowing that video would go out to the world, my husband and my daughter, Chelsea, were there. Chelsea said, "Mummy, I've never been more proud of you than when you stood in front of the judges and just took it!" I find this to be one of the best things any mother could hear.

Can I honestly say that I don't care what people think? It really depends on my mood, but I have found that over the years I care less and less. When I hear the victim or the judge within me, I just say, "Stop it." Like you, I have about 60,000 thoughts a day, and I do not want the victim and the judge in those thoughts.

**I love being on stage, working an audience,
but that feeling does not even come near to
the joy and gratitude I feel when I watch
people get out of pain. Tears of joy are the
best and that feeling is what inspired both
the documentary and this book. The goal is
to get you — dear reader, out of pain.**

What people who live from ego-love have that people who live from self-love don't is doubt. I'm not saying that people who love themselves don't have doubt.
Of course they do, but they deal with it by learning to
laugh at anxious thoughts. Instead, they get back in
touch with their intention by going inside, being grateful, and being kind to themselves first. That's really
the trick! If you can pattern interrupt anxious
thoughts by using these methods, very soon, you'll
begin to dream again. That's the way nature is.

**The faces of loving intention are:
self-love, grace, kindness, beauty,
forgiveness, abundance, expansiveness,
enthusiasm, humility, and a knowing within —
that you are on your spiritual journey of
service to others. The Laws of Nature are
the faces of loving intention.**

CHAPTER 29

Suffering in Silence
Dominique Shipstone

My journey from chronic pain to being pain free was a long one. I had attributed my pain to the three car accidents that I had been in — one when I was just ten years old, the other at age nineteen, and the last one when I was thirty-five. At the time of this writing, I am nearly 50 years old, and I have been pain free for eighteen months.

Of course I didn't know then what I know now. As I look back now, I very much believe that the pain I experienced was rooted in childhood trauma, and because of that trauma I had made some decisions in my life which were not the best for me. That said, I also believe I needed to make those decisions so that I would become sick and tired of being sick and tired and do something to heal — which is what happened. Those decisions gave me learnings which in turn allowed me to heal. Sometimes we go the long way around the houses. Could my path to healing have been faster? Maybe. Were those accidents no accident and instead a wake-up call?

I had tried almost everything to help my back pain. The only thing I never did was take pain killers. I didn't want to become dependent on a pill, and if I am honest, I think I wanted to suffer. Now that may sound strange, but because of the trauma in my young years, my unconscious belief about myself was not very good, and therefore I suffered — and did so quietly. I wasn't one to talk about the pain. I didn't complain or moan. I suffered in silence.

And there it is right there — suffering in silence, which was exactly what had happened with the child abuse. I never told anyone. Instead I lost my voice and I didn't find it fully until I was forty years old.

It was at forty that so much changed. I decided I was worth more than I was experiencing, and I started to heal.

By the time I found out about pain elimination, all of those past hurts were long resolved, and I had learned to love me. I believe that my body simply got stuck, or rather the pain energy was stagnant and stuck. It took under twenty minutes for me to become pain free. There was no unconscious resistance at all. It was simply a case of the unconscious understanding that old pain served no purpose and was totally unnecessary. It was the completion of my healing around what had happened all of those years ago. Mind and body freedom. The Soul got closure on that time in all ways.

I have learned that if I let day-to-day stresses mount up and I don't take notice of me, my body will give me a gentle warning shot — a twinge, a small reminder. I take care of that by going out in nature to be with my nature, to "be." After all we are human beings..."being," not doing!

Having healed and let go of the pain, I now enjoy helping others do the same. I believe that their unconscious/Soul knows that it is in good company. It's an unconscious knowing and trust — which along with my intention and the client's intention to be pain free, works — it just does!

We can become so used to pain that we don't really truly notice just how impactful it is on our lives. It's not until we decide to let go right now and that pain drains away, that everything becomes clear and the sun comes out again (metaphorically). When this happens, life changes completely, and as such, we do as well. Our vibration is where it was meant to be once more, and that allows for all kinds of miracles to take place. For me, I also found such deep gratitude for life, which I had lost whilst in pain.

I truly believe that we can raise our consciousness from passive awareness, which is what we have when we are in pain. What I mean by that is when we are aware of the pain but unaware that we can diminish it or really change it, because of our conditioning.

Whilst there is no need to even believe the process of pain removal or elimination, allowing your conscious to become actively aware and intending to be pain free is all that is really required, along with the same intention from the therapist.

I view this as Soul growth — and the Soul yearns for it. We were not born to suffer. We were born to experience and learn, not to be trapped in stagnation. Life flows...energy flows...just like a flowing river. If that river has a tree hanging down over it and the tree is catching debris from other things, the river would simply divert at some point until it could flow freely. It will change direction because just as in life, everything changes. So too the pain you have experienced changes, and life flows again — maybe in a slightly different direction, and always for the better.

You can go inside now and commune with your unconscious. First, thank it for keeping you alive all of these years and then ask, "What is it you need to learn, the learning of which will allow you to let go of this pain right now?" And then listen for the answer. When you've received the answer, you may also want to ponder the question, "When did you last show yourself compassion...deep compassion?"

We can become frustrated, annoyed, and angry with the pain and ourselves. That is a fear state, because that is what those emotions are. When we are caught in branches of fear, we simply don't heal. When we cultivate self-love and self-compassion, that is the perfect environment for healing, where the body can be relaxed and in flow, and that is where we raise our vibration.

CHAPTER 30

Injustice

"Nothing in the world can bother you as much as your own mind, I tell you. In fact, others seem to be bothering you, but it is not others. It is your own mind." - Dalai Lama

At the base of injustice is blame. However, the Laws of Nature don't do blame. The sad truth, and it's often hard to stomach, is that we are all responsible for our own feelings. If we need to take legal remedy for something then so be it, but in the end, our own feelings are not the fault of someone else. Your feelings are your feelings. It's not only courageous to drain those negative emotions away, it's an act of trust, surrender and self-forgiveness.

Many people have a general understanding that their thoughts really do become the events of their lives and are willing to let go of the ones they don't wish to manifest, and that too can be a gradual process.

Let's talk further about blame. Children unfortunately often blame themselves for the mistaken actions of their parents, and there is nothing more insidious and odious than child abuse. As I am writing this book, the subject of sexual assault is dominating the news with the confirmation of a new Supreme Court Justice. Whether he is guilty or innocent is not the point here. Let's talk about feelings instead! It feels like a scab that has been picked at and not allowed to heal — a wound has been exposed! With the testimony being broadcast on TV, so many women and men are reliving nightmares and unhealed wounds. Sexual assault is loathsome — an awful violation. It can lead to self loathing and berating, depression, acute anxiety, post traumatic stress, suicidal thoughts (and suicide) and chronic pain.

Lauren's Story

In the *Drain ThatPain* documentary, Lauren shared that she had been sexually assaulted as a four-year-old left at a babysitter's house. Since we filmed I have had two appointments with Lauren. In both appointments, I used the Drain ThatPain technique. Lauren had suffered with Post Traumatic Stress (PTS), panic attacks, depression, and anxiety. Happiness is new for Lauren. Part of her has felt afraid of being too happy because it's the precursor of something tragic. Lauren has had to let go of the fear of the unknown. I quote Lauren: "I am always worried that happiness is going to go away — but so far, it hasn't. I have been finding true happiness!"

So much of pain is the expectation of pain. The medical profession means well but passes on the belief of pain management to their patients, because that is what doctors have been taught and people are conditioned to believe. I've seen hundreds of people get out of pain — collectively in my audiences on stage, in person in my office, and mostly, connecting through my computer to my client's commuter. The effectiveness of the on-line connection is testament to the fact that we are all energetically connected.

Darren's story

One of the reasons that pain may linger is a sense of injustice. Car accidents are unfortunately far too common. The process of working with insurance companies is grueling under any circumstances, especially when one party has very little insurance. Of course there are well meaning lawyers available to help, but even still, often the outcome brings a huge loss in many aspects of life.

Darren is a humanitarian who works in Nashville as a filmmaker, holistic teacher, massage therapist, and yoga therapist. I met Darren through my stage agent, Doretta Pugh Osburn, who owns "Night Sky Entertainment" which provides entertainment to colleges and the military. The incredibly talented Gabriel Redding (who provided the sound and score for the *Drain ThatPain* documentary), and a multi-talented musician, took me to the opening of a documentary about bullying in Nashville a few years ago called,

Hear Me Now. Gabriel had created the musical score. It was on this visit that I met the creative team of Casting Life Films in Nashville, including: Mike Stryker (*Drain ThatPain* videographer/editor), Shanah Zigler (Co-Producer), and Darren Williams (*Drain ThatPain* director). Since I've known Gabriel and Doretta for ten years, I felt quite comfortable considering adding others from the Casting Life team to the *Drain ThatPain* documentary (it's important to be creatively safe in the artistic world with your friends).

So I called Darren and said "Darren, I want to make a movie, and I want you to direct..." (In retrospect, I'm not sure I said "direct," as I didn't even know what a director did at that stage!) Darren replied "I would love to help you, but I was in a car accident eighteen months ago and I have trouble with pain from a torn-meniscus in my knee. I also fear I've lost my film-making skills as I have brain fog and pain when I move. I also can't do math and I have no energy."

So Darren and I set up an appointment via Skype on July 17, 2017, which was his 50th birthday. As he says in the documentary, "That pain was gone. I have not had any pain since that date, and all she said was, 'When you open up your eyes you will be free from your pain.'

The pain for Darren was a sense of injustice. He had a car accident with a lady who had very little insurance. It's not easy in these situations, when a person is feeling "run-down," to deal with lawyers — and the sad truth is that this process can be very demeaning and difficult to bear for a person dealing with chronic pain. I've talked about adrenal glands and the perception of pain. Darren's adrenals were depleted at this point.

Within no time at all, Darren was back on his feet. He was able to exercise again, do yoga, and get back to his clients. We started filming in November when Darren reported that he was back to full health — and full health included his film-making skills and an end to brain fog! In the film he is shown leaping over a sandcastle on Myrtle Beach on the same left knee that had a torn meniscus. This is a very different path than what the medical profession suggested for Darren. Surgeons, because they are trained to do surgeries, naturally suggest surgery.

My experience is that people have surgeries because of chronic pain. If they did not have pain, they may not have surgeries. I was very glad to have surgery when I broke my Achilles some years back, but that was an acute attack — new pain. Darren's pain was chronic.

Our clients let go of chronic pain using Drain ThatPain. Once they let go of the pain, they are free to start a totally new life with a huge sense of gratitude. It is that gratitude that multiplies. The new loving energy that these people put out into the world is truly heartwarming, and Soul affirming.

CHAPTER 31

Surrender and Forgiveness

We talked about ego-love and self-love. Surrendering is allowing yourself to be not only the face of intention (self-love), but also the harbinger of the Laws of Nature — kind, truthful, compassionate, forgiving to yourself and others, beautiful, expansive, and allowing all aspects of abundance into your life — including financial.

Surrender is really allowing yourself to be in the present moment, and being so grateful for that gift of NOW. It's never been about "winners and losers" — it's learning something that you already have within you.

Surrender is sometimes thought of as "giving in." But here's the thing — when people "give in" by going inside, dreaming, listening to their bodies and following their intuition — the union of the body-mind with the higher self allows new information to be absorbed. Surrender facilitates the integration of mind, body and spirit — as you also recognize that you are the co-creator, from whence all happiness, joy, and manifestation flow.

"Giving in" is permitting the Universe to flow within you. It's feeling the peaceful moment in

a protected state, realizing that you were never alone, that you have always been loved, and there is no such thing as not being part of a creative loving Universe when you are an infinite being. What will you create that will enliven your passion and fulfill the need of your highest intention — and in so-doing, benefit our loving planet?

Surrender begins with forgiving yourself, showing compassion, and being kind to yourself. We all fight a battle with the inner judge and victim who poison our thoughts and keep us enslaved in a world of ego-love, fear, judgement, and self-importance — but that battle can be won.

**When you forgive yourself or someone else who you feel has wronged you, it's not to excuse the behavior, rather you acknowledge that's it's more important to be compassionate and kind to yourself, than to suffer needlessly by harboring negative emotions.
Forgiveness heals!**

Forgiveness is best understood as an exchange of energy. The Hawaiians call this Ho'oponopono, (to make right). This is based on an ancient Hawaiian Huna belief that we must make right with others in our thoughts. Ho'oponopono has evolved in western spirituality from both parties being present with a mediator, the Kahuna, into an energetic process without a Kahuna. Both parties sincerely say "I forgive you, please forgive me!" It's something you do in your head, in your imagination and the energy changes accordingly.

It's hard to live fully and freely if you are scared to die. Fear can produce the "I'm never going to die syndrome," and that's putting your head in the sand for your spiritual self — your Soul! Living life from a position of ego-love never brings happiness, as it's all about ego dominance rather than self-love.

Ego-love is always a "never enough" syndrome.

Mind Exercise - Your Destiny Appointment

So make an appointment with your destiny now. Go look at yourself in the mirror and take a long look. Do this standing as long as your health permits. Memorize this sentence and say it as you look in the mirror.

"I am an infinite being, and as I look into the eyes of my Soul, I know that my Soul is forever. I feel love and am here to make loving intention come true and 'bring heaven to earth' for everyone.

Listen to your heart. Always. Learn to recognize the increased warmth in your heart as you memorize these words.

Paradise is not a place but simply a state of consciousness. When you learn to go there, to that safe place in stressful times, you can actually feel that stress leave the body. Every day in the shower, surrender as you allow your mind to go inside as you feel grounded in the love of Mother Earth coming through your feet. In this grounded state, it's important every day to allow any negativity within your body to flow out of you.

Surrender as a Buddhist term means allowing your physical self to connect with your divine self by letting go of your ego and surrendering to the divinity of the moment — the NOW.

In the presence of truth, emotional pain dissolves. Truth is information and energy. Loving energy and intention can always replace the stuck energy of pain. If you think about it, you'll realize it has to be true as it's a Law of Nature. When you surrender and let go of ego-love, the result is transformation! Yes, it's miraculous what happens when people let go of emotional pain, and then what they can create together.

As you progress spiritually, you understand the power of working with other creative people. It's what you can do together that's so miraculous. You are able to feel protected where in the past you might have felt threatened. Also, you have a sense of telepathic communication with your spiritual friends, who also change as you open yourself up to higher levels of consciousness.

The transformation energy of surrender reminds us that we gain so much more when we detach from micromanaging our dreams and allow in other energy, as we let the Universe direct how those dreams come true.

Besides, it never worked anyway when we tried to have the conscious reins!

It's also going to be so much more dramatic and un-believable than our own conscious attempts. Phew — what a relief!

People frequently get to a place of surrender, be-cause they are worn out. They are sick and tired of being sick and tired.

Cliff's story

When I met Cliff and his wife Billie in person in Myrtle Beach, they had suffered eight years of Cliff's pain. Billie never left his side for more than an hour. It started in his gut. He had six surgeries in eight years, and after every surgery, things got worse. Even when Cliff's colon was removed, he still had gut pain. Cliff was suicidally depressed and Billie was hanging onto the only thread she knew — knowing and pray-ing that her husband could be free of pain. She intu-itively knew that Cliff's pain was emotionally based. "He hangs onto pain," she said.

As you recall earlier in this book, I met Cliff and Bil-lie through Hillary Evans, a talented hypnotherapist in Charleston who referred me to them. After one Skype session with me, Cliff was pain free — but the pain returned in a lessened form. The good news is that I knew I had Cliff's attention. He was learning that when he could inhabit the pain and learn the truth of the message, the pain would go away.

Pain dissipates in the face of truth!

I decided to go and see Cliff in Myrtle Beach. I would then continue the drive to Nashville, where we were doing the majority of the filming for the *Drain ThatPain* documentary. When the Universe wants things to line up, it happens in extraordinary ways. Serendipitously, FedEx arrived with my Canon XC10 video camera just as I was leaving my driveway. I knew I could assist Cliff out of pain, and I wanted to film it. Of course, I'd never used the camera before! As I returned to the house, I remembered that my iPhone had crashed, so I needed some music to play for the drive. All I could find was a CD of Barbra Streisand's "Greatest Love Songs!"

When I arrived in Myrtle Beach that night at my beachfront Airbnb, I unwrapped the Amazon package, charged the Canon camera batteries, and loaded the SD cards. The next day, I arrived at 9:00 am at Cliff and Billie's house.

I haven't seen pain like that since my mother. Cliff was in such severe pain that he could neither hear me nor focus. He seemed to stay sane by alternately soaking his body in buckets of cold ice, followed by a hot shower.

Billie and I had time to learn how to use and set up the camera, or rather she did as she is a wiz at these kinds of things.

Eventually, things calmed down and we had the session around noon. As we started the session, I was thinking that I had never wanted anything so much as getting Cliff out of pain. He had an out of body experience (OBE), as he remembered injustice dissociated from afar in a prior life. I remember talking to him about a songbird that was free to fly and it was then as if the Universe shifted somehow and a songbird actually did begin to sing in a tree outside the window, right where we were working — a moment of pure grace.

When Cliff came back into his body all the pain had gone. It was a magical moment — a songbird's note "frozen in time!" And that songbird sang and sang and we all cried tears of joy in an unforgettably life-changing and life-affirming moment.

A person transforms from being a prisoner to a songbird (thank you Barbra Streisand) and that is the message of pain elimination. Billie got the first film on my Canon XC10. Since it passed our videographer, Mike Stryker's, brilliant standards, we used it in the documentary.

Cliff and I have had one session since then. During the last year, Cliff has become stronger and stronger mentally and physically. He's renewed his driver's license, and I was heartened to see pictures of him moving around boarding up his family and friend's houses with the approach of Hurricane Florence.

CHAPTER 32

Out of Body Experiences (OBE)

I got your attention on the last page with the phrase "OBE," didn't I? At this point maybe you are thinking, "This is a little woo woo for me." Let me assure you that you can *Drain ThatPain* without leaving your body. An OBE is by no means a precursor to draining that pain.

However, the ability to visualize our bodies and see ourselves in the picture is a very powerful tool. This ability is found in more recently evolved mammals with more highly developed frontal lobes (cerebral lobes) in the brain. Some examples of these animals include: chimpanzees, whales, dolphins, and elephants.

For some people, an OBE is seeing yourself in the picture (dissociation) — like watching a movie of yourself. It's akin to lucid dreaming — that half awake feeling! When you are having an OBE or a lucid dream, you are aware that you are dreaming and you feel yourself in a different place, maybe a different time. The key is that you see yourself in the picture. Your Soul is still in your earthly body.

**Now, when the Soul leaves the body —
that's akin to the peanut leaving the shell.
At that point, you are either dead
(transformed) or astral traveling!**

Visualization combined with inspiration motivates the body-mind and makes the whole process so much more dynamic. This is effective goal setting. If your goal, for example, is fitness and weight loss, it's powerful to see yourself with a smile on your face, feeling pumped up, wearing those skinny jeans (you know the ones you've always rocked), waiting for you at the back of the closet!

All it takes is a decision to let go of the emotional pain in your body that has been protecting you. It's easy then to set the intention, and then to see yourself out there where you belong — on center stage in those jeans!

You have given your body-mind direction, and the NAV system hones in on that end result. The rudder is set on the boat and your body-mind. Manifestation is inevitable.

When you look at things from a different perspective — when you put a "new frame on a picture" — it changes the meaning of the picture. Drain ThatPain has you floating back above your time line to the origin of the feeling behind the chronic pain.

In many cases, the event in your time line might have been the acute attack (initial sensitizing event) of chronic pain.

The underlying predominant emotion, however, could be sadness, guilt, anger, fear, or doubt (a limiting belief), and that's what we are looking for!

It's not a conscious thing; it's an unconscious thing. That feeling could be in the womb or a previous lifetime. During your session, you'll have a sense of knowing about what it is — it'll just pop into your head. Suppose the issue is self-esteem. If a client has a first event for "not feeling good enough" before birth, I'll ask, "How many lifetimes ago?" The client will just "blurt" out a number. That's it! It's the first thing that comes to mind. Never doubt it — it's trusting your body-mind.

Your Intuition Talking

An OBE can feel otherworldly — like the "Tesla Tug" in my spine, or goosebumps! The feeling that comes with it is that of heightened sensory intelligence — a gift!

Trust and thank that voice. It often comes at an unexpected time in an unexpected way. It can be a whisper followed by a dramatic silence. It can come in the form of a random song, or it can be overheard in a supermarket soundtrack as you reach for something you want. It happens to me most when I'm outside and doing something repetitive — movement stimulates it.

There is nothing like a hike to activate the creative juices or, indeed, raking leaves (I'm not a fan of the leaf blower, as it's noisy). For me, it's being outside. I believe that wisdom comes right out of the soil. Whenever possible, I go barefoot. I love to feel the ground on my feet — it's a level of spiritual connectedness.

One thing is for sure, the Universe is always giving you messages. It's never a matter of whether the messages are there or not, but rather — are you open to receive them? Keep saying "Yes" to new messages that resonate. Remember messages can be received through sound, visually, by feelings, tastes, or hunches.

Your job is to open up your mind, open up your senses, and be grateful. Gratitude is always there with its Soulmate — joy! It's about making a conscious decision to recognize, honor, and be grateful. And of course — it's really about love.

So many people become depressed from chronic pain. It's important to remember to open the curtains, go outside, and be in nature as much as you can. Nature reminds us that the Universe is abundant and endlessly beautiful. Reflect that! Be that beauty — be that truth, because truth is beauty and beauty is truth. Set a goal to let go of your pain permanently. Read this book with that intention. And keep reading — it's made as a spiritual bedtime book — something to read that slows you down and opens up your mind.

Along with visualizing yourself outside your body comes the enhanced empathy

found in more evolved mammals.

To be able to see ourselves in a story makes us more empathetic as humans. We learn from stories. However, sometimes the stories that we tell ourselves are the most damaging.

Our stories, whether real or imagined are our perceptions. I like to think that it's never too late to have a happy childhood. Telling yourself wonderful real or imagined stories, staying grounded in the moment, and honoring yourself allows you to slow it all down and open your awareness. That's enough to banish anxiety. Then the magic happens — you dream! Remember that is what you are here to do on this planet.

Look for the beauty in all things and become the face of intention by reflecting that beauty back into the world. The Universe simply wants to know the end result, the zip code on the GPS. Enjoy the ride!

CHAPTER 33

Furtive Glances

Now, I have never been to the Arctic
But I have seen pictures
Of baby seals with white fuzzy coats
Camouflaged against the inhospitable Arctic ice
And the hungry eyes of a polar bear
It is nature's way to protect the young
Lions have their cubs
In the summertime
When the tundra grows
And the cubs can play safely in the grass
Under the radar of a hyena
Every so often the cubs make furtive glances
Above the grass
To check that mother is nearby
So they can continue playing safely
And the baby seals grow
Obtain their adult coats
Designed for swimming
Because nature knows
When the correct time is
To leave the nest
To swim alone
To leave the pride behind
The time for protection is over
Freedom and growth are born

A knowing in every animal
Whether parent or offspring
That the time is right
For a change
Now no one ever said
That it was easy to let go
To leave security behind
To move on
And we can create a special place
In our mind's eye
Where we feel safe and secure
Some people create a private niche
A hammock in the garden
To celebrate their alone time
To enjoy their privacy
To meditate
My friend has a womb room
Decorated with plush thick carpeting
In dark colors with plenty of wood
And lots of books all the way
To the ceiling
Intimate lighting
A place to listen to music
Dedicated to relaxation
To feel the pulse of life
To feel safe and protected in your own world

CHAPTER 34

Tesla and the Vortex

"Create the drain!" These were the words of Shanah Zigler, the co-producer of the documentary. We did create the drain filming at some fabulous waterfalls near Nashville. I'm grateful for Shanah — she did so much for the movie. Not only did she give creative advice, she's also an actress in several of the scenes, worked cameras and sound, did my makeup, and advised on wardrobe. Even her dog, Heidi, made an appearance in the film!

Creating the drain is creating the vortex. Metaphorically, the Universe is like a giant vortex and your experience on this planet will depend on how close you get to the flow. When you are in the flow, your dreams manifest, you have heightened sensory awareness, and you don't have anxiety, doubt or chronic pain. You feel peaceful and in harmony with your body, mind, and Soul. Body, Mind, Soul.

Tesla captured the free energy from Niagara Falls, and his alternating current (AC) became the norm. He was fascinated (and still is) with the numbers 3,6,9 as well as nature's symbols, shapes and patterns that occur in galaxies — all natural processes. One of these patterns is the hexagon that can commonly be found in the honeycomb, for example. Math is the basis of these patterns and is believed to be sacred code — sacred geometry!

Imagine planet Earth as a giant vortex with the axis of the North and South Pole being the middle. The middle of the vortex is the core, the drain, and yes — the free energy. Your thoughts!

In vortex math, there is a pattern that repeats itself: 1, 2, 4, 8, 7, and 5, and so on 1, 2, 4, 8, 7, 5, 1, 2, 4, 8, 7, 5, 1, 2, 4...

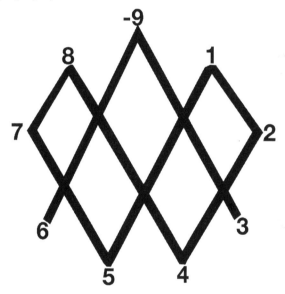

3, 6, and 9 are in a triangular pattern. Whereas 5,7, and 8 on one side are exchanging energy with 1,2 and 4.

Now when you start doubling 3 you get 6 and if you double that you get 12, 24, 48 etc. None of these numbers are divisible by 9. There is no mention of 9. It's outside the pattern. It's the free energy,thought, creation itself. 9 is the symbol for enlightenment. It's the top of the Pyramid, the tip of the triangle (metaphorically body, mind and Soul) — the flux energy inside the vortex leading to a higher dimension. Tesla calls this tuning into another frequency.

So when you create the vortex (the Drain), your body-mind follows the metaphor. You then allow the 9 energy — the new energy — into your body, as rainbows of light balance your energy chakras as the pain drains. Why do we do this? Because nature abhors a vacuum. I believe that you must fill that person up with hope, expectation and enthusiasm. Metaphorically this is the new light. When you are up above your life on your time line and looking out at your fabulous future, the pain will drain because the loving energy is stronger than the fear. Truth and beauty dissolve fear.

"The day science begins to study non-physical phenomena, it will make more progress in one decade than in all the previous centuries of its existence." — Nikola Tesla

Tesla is interested in telepathy. *Tele* meaning distance and *pathy* meaning healing. I have felt Tesla's familiar tug in some training sessions, where I train a therapist and a client (in pain) at the same time on Skype. We metaphorically create a triangle – therapist, client and myself – and we take this beautiful triangle which is our Souls' (higher selves) into an etheric crystalline pyramid. Then, inside the pyramid, we download the necessary information for our cells to increase our extrasensory perception. Some might call this going to another dimension. Awakening! When you ask and set intention, you receive. The result is a sense of pure bliss, peacefulness. It leaves the person after the session with a light-floating-feeling of connectedness. It's so powerful for healing, and you feel like you are tasting heaven before your time (hey — there is no time!) and all fear is gone. You establish a very peaceful, safe place that your body can return to at any time. As Robin would say – ("it's a feather bed, Baby..!)"

So we want to be able to measure telepathy at every level and that includes microscopic. I've bought a microscope so I can look at cells, water crystals at 2500x magnification. Our cells have a consciousness and their own Souls. When we sing harmony to our Souls and bathe them in love and gratitude, we feel uplifted. Water is our external self, and it mirrors our emotions. Can we use water crystals to distribute, measure healing? Tesla is believed to have established nodal points for 3,6,9 energy for earth. Can we tap into these central points using channeling, telepathy and heal millions of people?

You may remember that I talked about the sacred tribe, the Kogis of the Amazon basin and their amazing skills in channeling and ability to achieve *Aluna* or enlightenment. Can we learn further from the Kogis, who have google-mapped every tree on their sacred mountain and apparently have their own energetic maps of the world? What can we learn from the combined wisdom of the Kogis and Tesla?

There is an interesting phenomena called "morphic resonance," a term coined by the British researcher, Rupert Sheldrake, as a form of collective inherent memory in nature at the cellular level. Glycerin, for example never used to freeze and form crystals. Then one day, glycerin for no apparent reason froze. It didn't just happen in one container of glycerin. It happened in glycerin all over the world. Can morphic resonance help us understand precognition, telepathy? Experiments done with dogs suggest that dogs know intuitively when their owners are leaving their offices and coming home! Now morphic resonance is not uniformly accepted by the scientific community, but it is certainly of interest to me, the mind-body community and anyone studying natural energetic phenomena.

We live in exciting times. I'm optimistic about the future of Mother Earth. I certainly want to do my part to advance the belief that pain elimination can be achieved worldwide, and I'm happy to be a subject of anyone else's research.

CHAPTER 35

The River Stone Fountain

I've reproduced here the last 10 minutes of the documentary. Follow along and feel the energy in your body. You can do this with your eyes open or closed.

I am happy to be here.
And I invite you to take this opportunity to
Just close your eyes
And if it's the right time for you
Let go of anything that you need to let go of
So that when you leave here today
You can absolutely embrace your fabulous life
You can do this with your eyes open or closed
And I'm going to feel the energy come in
Through my feet
And bring that energy
Up now in my knees and into my body
And up into my heart and feel that heart expand
Green
And then up into my throat
So I say the things that I need to say
And into my face - my pineal gland -
The center of my intuition
And then again, the top of my head
So breathe in again and feel
That energy come up again

Joanna Cameron

Coming up through your body and then
Down out through your hands
And one more time
And as I sit here in the mist
I feel that water on my skin
I can see the light reflect off the mist
Creating rainbows of light
And now feel it in your body
As it trickles thru every cell
Fiber of your body
Washes you totally clean
Feel that just like the river stone fountain
Those beautifully smooth rounded river stones
Ground down by time and water
And see it trickle all the way down
Through your body
Cleansing and healing every nerve, muscle,
Fibre, molecule
Even the space between the atoms - the quarks
All the way down
And as it does that the new energy comes in
I feel that right now coming in through my body
Down through my legs and out of my feet
So that metaphorically when I leave this place
Which maybe I never really do in my mind
We can leave behind anything
Today
Limiting decisions, doubts
Make the decision today
Intend
To live your life

Completely in the moment
So that moment expands
So that you see new things
That your intuition opens up
Negative thoughts are gone in that state
Make the decision to do that
So as all of that drains through your body
When you open up your eyes
Your awareness will be open
And everything looks different
As you get on with this moment
As you attend to the present
But intend for the future
So allow your eyes to open
When everything has been resolved
And you know you feel
Fabulous

We've learned to expend energy that is not needed. Loving intention alone can be enough to let go of pain. Surrender a little bit to allow the Universe in. That's where the magic happens. Let Go. Your spirit will come alive as your new life opens in unbelievably beautiful exciting ways. And feel the ripple effect go out into the world. And the goosebumps remind you that we have one heart, we are not alone!

**And what will you do
with loving intention
to heal the World...?**

CHAPTER 36

The Angel Metatron

I am the Angel Metatron, the Peace Angel and someone you need to know. You see, Angels are always with you but because we're Angels – we don't necessarily come into your life unless invited. So invite me! I am an Angel who has lived on earth in mortal form and I can sincerely relate about inhumanity and suffering. I am genuinely sorry! But please know that I am an Angel of Peace, who helps you with emotional inner conflict because my job is to record all the thoughts of the Universe in the Akashic records. That way we can check on the health of the Universe. So let me help you with your thoughts. I can give you signs when you are on the right intuitive track. You're going to love them! So just allow your awareness to open up to allow that to happen.

Now, as the Angel Metatron – I am known for my metatron cube. Did you know that within that cube is every sacred pattern, and all, of course abide by the Laws of Nature. So allow yourself to imagine that metatron cube with you in space, floating above the earth. And when you enter these sacred patterns within the cube – first, the cells of your body and then 2500x further magnified into the crystal geometry, the hexagon, the divine geometry soothes you. It's like plugging yourself into bright white divinity light. It's as if you are watching your own godliness (higher self). You feel a sense of oneness, and you know you have always belonged. And your body downloads this sacred program so that when you open up your eyes, not now, but in a few moments, you know you feel different, lighter, enlightened and the moment has expanded! You have effectively bathed the core of your self in love, and that always produces harmony in nature.

You will notice below, I appeared in Joanna's fireplace! So peace, love and harmony to you. I'm grateful for you and I hope that you reflect and ripple that gratitude into the world. You rock more good!

CHAPTER 37

Drain ThatPain — Melbourne, Australia
Benetta Wainman

Why do we do the job we do? I decided to train to drain away people's pain, because pain elimination is immensely personal and very important to me. You see, my own brother committed suicide because of his chronic pain. It took away his self esteem and his confidence, and caused him to stop being the person he was. If only someone like myself was there to help him to understand that the pain was there mainly because of the emotions he was feeling. If only he had the support for that, instead of being told the only solution was to have yet another operation that involved him living without most of his bowel, and having a bag attached to him. He was such a private person and really hated everything about his illness, but it was the constant pain that drove him to do what he did. He left a grieving wife, two broken daughters, and a mother who never really got over the fact that her son took his own life — let alone died before her. Chronic pain causes devastation. If I can do anything to stop even one person from suffering, then I will.

Remembering back, I think I always had a psychic ability. My childhood wasn't particularly happy or sad, though I remember much happiness through time spent with family and friends. We always had people around us, and my mother always made the best of everything. She never once made us feel poorly done by. I am very grateful for her and how she taught me how to love, give, and be truly grateful for everything.

It was at the age of nineteen, I think, when I was first introduced to hypnosis by a team of people wanting to prove that we had existed before, by choosing a small number of people who replied to an advertisement in the local paper. When I regressed to another lifetime and was asked questions, it almost felt like I was acting, however. The voice wasn't at all like mine, and the things she said were not mine. It was as if I had been fed those words. Though I had my doubts, there was something that struck me about the process. During the session, there was a transition to another life through a gate in a walled garden. As I opened the gate a magnificent yellow light engulfed me, and I felt nothing but pure love. That feeling stayed with me and still to this day makes me believe that our Souls are full of light and love, if we allow it in.

My career as a nurse began not too long after this, and my life of caring and deep empathy for humans began. Though being empathetic and caring were a part of my career, I know that I've always looked for the deeper emotions that existed beyond presenting issues, and that permeated the next thirty years of my life, no matter what I did for "work." That is until one day something changed. My world started to fall apart when my wonderful, deeply affectionate boy became sick. His illness continued long after his father and I thought it would. Instead of getting better and more resilient — his world fell apart too. He became unhappy, dissociated himself from his world, lost his close friends and girlfriend, and changed so much I didn't feel like I knew him anymore. He was in so much pain that he turned to alcohol in order to numb everything out. All his hopes and expectations started to fade, and with it went his self-esteem and confidence, as he became physically weak with little or no interest in anything. I don't think it helped that his younger sister was so outgoing and was starting to excel in all academic fields and travel the world. This shattered my husband and my world, leaving us at a loss as to how to help him.

It was at this time that I discovered hypnotherapy. I had already become interested in looking at holistic and natural healing methods, but what really pushed me was that I had a son that was hurting, and I was going to do ANYTHING to help him get through this. Little did I know at that time that no matter what I wanted, it was he alone that could change things and he alone that could make the decision for when and how it was going to happen. My training was fast as I not only had to be prepared for Sam to make that decision, but also because this modality of healing hit me big time. In my second training course we did an exercise where you ask all of the parts of you to come together and become whole (parts integration). I asked my inner Soul, "Who am I meant to be — Nurse or Hypnotherapist?" The answer I received was clear — my calling was to heal people through hypnotherapy. I literally cried with joy and relief at having discovered a modality that fit me completely.

Although I was relieved to have discovered my true career path, now I had to find a niche that also fit with my values. I tried smoking cessation — no, that wasn't it. Weight loss — I did very well at this, even having people travel from Sydney to see me, but that still didn't seem to be it. I was still having trouble finding my niche when on a particular day I saw a post about a MeetUp that I had been attending sporadically. At this particular MeetUp, a lady named Joanna Cameron was going to come to talk to our group of fellow hypnotherapists about something called Drain ThatPain. I had watched Joanna before this on Facebook Live with Helen Mitas. She intrigued me with her bubbly personality and vibrancy, and it was a sure sign to me that I had to go.

Immediately after meeting her in person I also knew that I had to do the practitioner training. The only drawback was that four days from then I would be traveling to Greece with my daughter — the day after the training. I had heaps to do, but I am sure you know how this story goes. Sure enough, I was one of the lucky people to take Joanna's training. From that day on I released pain wherever and whenever I could. There was no stopping me. Once I understood that chronic pain could be eliminated, quickly and easily, and all that was needed was intention, I was amazed. All I could think about was how many people could live again. People like my poor brother, who had taken his own life because of chronic pain, could be free.

To have the freedom of choice, to live however they desire — whether that be an exceptional life or just to be happy with their lot doesn't matter — but to have freedom to see the light of day, wake up and know without a doubt that they were pain free. Now that was something — something that made my heart sing!

Now each day I allow my heart to sing, my Soul to grow, and my energetic field to shine. I know that Joanna was heaven sent, and that I am an angel on Earth sent to help people to heal. I was told by Helen Lloyd, a kinesiologist, that I was sent by Archangel Metatron to do this work and to heal. At the time, this freaked me out a bit, as I had only just started doing hypnotherapy. However, she seemed very impressed and slightly in awe of me. When I learned more about Archangel Metatron, I knew I had some big shoes to fill — and at my age, fifty-nine at the time, I felt that time was ticking already. Since then I have gone further than I ever thought possible, and I know this is just the beginning of my adventure. I do this work for my brother, my mother who could have been saved the terrible anguish of having her son die before her (something I think she didn't really get over), and for my son who is still with me and pushes me when I have those days of a "too hard basket." Most of all though — I do it for all those people who want to be free.

CHAPTER 38

Getting to a True Zero
Amanda Dobra Hope

How do you get far enough underneath the present-ing issue to eliminate the physical or emotional pain completely? If you choose to see a Drain ThatPain practitioner, it helps if they are tuned in to their intu-ition and well versed in the practice of masterfully holding space in order to guide you to that place as quickly as possible. No matter how skilled they are, however, I do find that it's possible for a complete re-lease of physical or emotional pain to take more than one session to get down to a true zero, depending on how much healing work you have done on the issue previously. (This is further supported by Joanna's ex-planation that the body-mind will never leave you com-pletely unprotected, as its chief job is to protect you).

As I am a holistic life coach, author, writer, and speaker, the clients who are naturally drawn to me tend to be those in emotional pain. You may remem-ber Beth, Ashley, and Tavarus in the documentary. These are my clients, and in full disclosure, also my friends. They were all in emotional pain.

Beth had a history of extreme shame that was not hers to carry that she knew was blocking her from moving ahead in her life and career. Though she leads a large group for creatives and is well known as a community builder and artist in her community, she still felt as if she was held back by the shackles of shame in her every endeavor. Beth graciously agreed to be filmed while I was doing a Drain ThatPain session on her, and was astounded by how free she felt afterwards. Though she is also a friend of mine, I am very mindful to hold all of my clients in the greatest love and safety as I work with them, and I make sure that they can feel that. Beth knew she could trust me, and that even though we were on camera, I would not push her anywhere too vulnerable, or speak out loud any of her private information that came up in the session barring her being the one to offer it. This safety and trust is imperative in Drain ThatPain. When a client knows their practitioner can hold a strong energetic container in love and genuine concern for their emotional safety, the session will have a much greater chance of producing maximum results.

Ashley had been to more than one doctor for chronic physical pains. It was a wake-up call to her when they all asked her (within the same general time frame) if she had ever considered that her pain might be emotional in origin. Ashley and I had two sessions in my office. The first went as a normal session would. In the second, however, some amazing things happened as I allowed my intuition to guide me, and felt the spiritual assistance we were being given. In allowing this spiritual assistance (which doesn't always happen), it was as if I was being helped to put all of her "pieces" back together again. What came through in

Ashley's session was that she was fragmented; that all of the aspects of her being were not working to-gether in harmony. After the second session, her life literally opened up. The next time I saw her, she just about trampled me with excitement and hugs as I walked through the door, so excited to tell me about everything that started moving forward in her per-sonal life and career. Since that day, so many things she had previously been toiling away at and hoping for in her life have come to fruition, and the train is still rolling full speed ahead into manifestation-land! Ashley owns a successful art gallery in Nashville, is an artist agent, and has made some pretty impressive projects come to life including facilitating the instal-lation of one of Beth's paintings screen-wrapped around a city bus!

Tavarus had come to me with the feeling of loneli-ness. Through our session, he was able to trace that feeling back to something completely benign that hap-pened when he was a child. He had not actually been "shut out" emotionally from his father because there was something undesirable about him, but rather his father had shut the door to try to protect him. For years though, his body-mind could only remember the loneliness he felt, something his father probably never would have been able to anticipate, as you can never tell how someone else might process something emo-tionally, especially when your intentions are good.

CHAPTER 39

Emotional Fitness
"21st Century: Exciting
Times for Change"
Carol Robertson, PhD

Recent discoveries about the activity in our brains have been compared to being as exciting as exploring our Universe. Through this work we now have important new insights into our emotions, our behaviors, and human flexibility. Our ability to learn and change is described well with the term "neuroplasticity." Plasticity here means "able to change," moldable — like the process of forming a sculpture. Whenever neurons link or delink, a cascade of responses also occurs. These may be experienced as new emotional responses, behaviors, abilities, and ultimately beliefs about ourselves. Scientists say that our new knowledge about our flexibility will change how we approach medicine, education, wellness, and everyday living for the better.

This century the speed of change can be hyperfast. This very new information has already helped in the generation of psychosensory methods which are believed to facilitate both the linking and delinking of neural pathways. These techniques have been honed to be pleasant and easy to use and are grounded in biology, neuroscience, human creativity, and behaviors. All that is required is the knowledge of how to use them. This means that, once learned, they can be used anywhere and cost nothing to use.

Worldwide, people have been using this knowledge to help them recover from the after effects of experiencing traumatic events such as: PTSD, chronic pain, anger, anxieties, fears, rage or unwanted thoughts, memories, feelings, ideas, or sensory overwhelm.

People have also been using psychosensory processes to become calmer, to reach their goals, and to learn more easily. After experiencing a set of specially designed techniques, many people have expressed that they felt that they were now in a "safe haven," and so these processes have become known as the Havening Techniques®. Now the idea of sculpting our neurology with the aim of emotional fitness can be added alongside what we already know about physical fitness and caring well for ourselves.

My dream is that every schoolchild will be taught about this science and the Havening Techniques,® which were created and developed by Dr. Ronald Ruden and Dr. Steven Ruden. Their team of trainers are sharing the information around the world with therapists, medical professionals, first responders, teachers, and individuals interested to learn for their own use. Certified practitioners can be found on the official website www.havening.org. The fastest way to learn about Havening Techniques is to work with a certified Havening practitioner, or attend a training if you would like to become a certified practitioner of the Havening Techniques. I also have developed animal-assisted Havening Techniques, and these gentle methods are relaxing for both the animals and the people. There are many techniques and uses, so do feel free to contact me to find out more at www.psychosensoryacademy.com and explore the official Havening website to read more, see upcoming training information, and find a practitioner near you.

These following example scenarios show how our brains learn and how Havening is being used. In each example I have used the same sensory information to demonstrate how the same element can trigger happy memories for some people and anxiety for others.

Scenario One

A person experiences an event they find very distressing, meaningful and inescapable; it's sunny and a particular tune is heard (adrenaline and cortisol are released and a neural pathway is generated in the amygdala).

Some months later, out with friends eating ice cream, they hear the tune again. The neural pathway is activated and similar brainwaves and chemistry are experienced, and the unpleasant information related to the memory is experienced as a flashback image, noise or feeling. The person starts to cry and explains to friends what they are remembering about the distressing event. The neural pathway is strengthened, and the information about this event is added.

A few days later the weather is sunny and the person feels stressed (adrenaline and cortisol are released). When friends invite the person out, they cannot face it and say no. The person is now in their sympathetic system which is designed to help us survive stressful events. The person now starts to form a belief that they are not coping and want to be on their own, indoors and away from the sun.

The person contacts a Havening practitioner for help. The practitioner guides them through a special process called Event Havening, which involves very lightly activating the unpleasant memory for a minute. The Havening Touch is used by the practitioner to generate delta waves as they guide the person to think pleasant thoughts for around five to ten minutes. This is believed to enable the neural pathway to delink. To check if the process has been successful the person attempts to activate the neural pathways formed during the unpleasant or traumatizing experience and finds that they now have a calmer response. After the session the testing continues as the person notices how they feel about trips out with friends in the sun, responses when the tune is heard, or when ice cream is seen, smelled or tasted.

Scenario Two

A person experiences an event they find fun; it's a sunny day and a particular tune is heard (serotonin, endorphins and oxytocin are released and a neural pathway is generated).

Some days later, out with friends eating ice cream,

they hear the same tune. The neural pathway is activated and similar brainwaves and chemistry are experienced. The person starts to smile and explains to their friends what they are remembering about the happy event (the neural pathway is strengthened and the information about this event is added).

A few days later the person is in a very stressful situation (adrenaline and cortisol are released), and to calm down and feel resourceful they use a Havening Technique to help them manage. To begin, the Havening Touch generates delta brainwaves and they begin to feel calmer. Then using Ifformational Havening Technique (which is designed to activate helpful neural pathways and electrochemistry) they deliberately begin to think about being in that wonderful place, enjoying eating ice cream and listening to that particular tune. Having altered their own electrochemistry, they start to think about "what if things improved," as they remember what resources they have and what can happen if they tap into their skills, sense of humor, and flexibility. This chemistry of serotonin, endorphins, and oxytocin helps them move into their parasympathetic system in a matter of minutes. As a result of using the Ifformational Havening technique, they feel calmer and more resourceful, and they often even see a funny side to the situation.

CHAPTER 40

Creating 'Laser-like' Thoughts that Heal
Randi Light

Did you know that we have 60,000 thoughts a day and the electrical impulses of our thoughts can be measured with an EEG? Author and poet, Rumi Da, states that our thoughts have a 'laser-like' power and that thoughts can be pulsed. What does he mean by laser and how can we give our thoughts the power to heal? The term "laser" originated as an acronym for "light amplification by stimulated emission of radiation." I tend to think of laser as hyper-focused. This chapter is about how and why to add enough energy to our thoughts to heal our bodies, minds, and Souls in order to create our best self and life.

It's been scientifically proven that our thoughts can heal the physical body, our bodies and other people's bodies, too. Check out this study. There was an experiment done by Doctors Marilyn Schlitz & William Braud. In this experiment they put human red blood cells in a test tube along with a saline solution that had enough salt in it to kill the cells. Their participants in the study were able to focus their minds and protect the cells from bursting open!

Not every single thought has a 'laser-like' power.

There are specific things we can 'do' that makes thought stronger or the pulse more intense. One thing we can do is add a heightened emotion of love, joy or appreciation to something we want.

Dr. Glenn Rein, one of the main researchers for The Institute for HeartMath conceived of a study to test healers' ability and their effects on biological systems. In Dr. Rein's experiment, all participants had been trained in creating heart coherence and getting into an elevated mood of love, joy or appreciation which can be measured. Also, all participants were holding vials of DNA suspended in deionized water.

The first group in the study were told to enter into an elevated mood and see if it had any effect on the vials of DNA they were holding. Upon analysis of those samples, no statistically significant changes had occurred in the DNA.

A second group held a clear intent to change the DNA, but they were to NOT enter into a positive emotional state. This group had no statistically significant changes to the DNA samples.

A third group of trained participants were told to enter into the elevated mood of love, joy or appreciation AND simultaneously hold a clear intention to either wind or unwind the strands of DNA. This group produced statistically significant changes in the shape of the DNA samples. The DNA was wound or unwound as much as 25% in some cases.

The key point here is that is in order to produce an intended effect you must be in an elevated mood of love, joy or appreciation AND focus on the outcome you want. In essence, an intentional thought needs an energizer or a catalyst like heightened emotions. Another way of summing this up and what I teach all my clients is to:

Vividly Imagine the end result with a great feeling!

A key component is to get crystal clear on the outcomes you want. Even if the outcome you want is to know what you want. You are creating a clear intention of something you want to have, be, feel, learn, accept, achieve, or experience. The second key is to pretend that you already have these results. Picture the outcomes in your mind with as many details as possible – hear the sounds around you and your thoughts.

Feel how good it feels to have this outcome. Some of you may be able to smell the smells or taste the tastes of this mind-movie of your end results.

According to Dr. Potswami, if you hold the thought (image) for 17 seconds, it's like making a phone call to the quantum field. Or you could say it's like sending a clear message of what you want to the Intelligence that created you, your Higher Self, God, Source, Spirit, your Angels, Guides and all parts of you. Infinite possibilities are the hallmark of the quantum field. In that field, you are healed and happy. Can you imagine being in the field with the outcomes you want already in place? Use all your senses. How do you act, think and feel when you are no longer in pain? Really get into it for a minimum of 17 seconds. Keep in mind that 17 seconds is longer than you think. You might want to time yourself at first to give you an idea. Practice, practice, practice. Do you think holding a thought or image for 17 seconds gives it a laser like power and provides a clear message that this is important? Yep!

Furthermore, there are specific times in your day that make it easier for you to visualize and materialize your intentions. Specifically, when you are going to sleep and waking up in the morning. When you are falling asleep your brain waves start to slow down from Beta into Alpha, Theta and then Delta which is sleep. The same thing happens in the morning only as you awaken your brain waves leave Delta and go into Theta, Alpha and then Beta. When your brain waves are cycling in Alpha and Theta you are in a hypnotic state in which you are more open and receptive. The Institute for Cognitive and Neuroscience discovered that a suggestion given in a hypnotic state, even one time can have the same effect as long term conditioning and practice. The suggestions can be from you or from an audio recording. What you are doing or saying as you fall asleep affects how you sleep and how you feel when you wake up in the morning.

I had the pleasure of interviewing Life Coach, Mike Sassorossi on my Facebook live show called *The Randi Light Experience*. One of my favorite quotes from Mike that came through him is an affirmation to assist in changing B.S. That stands for BS, but it also stands for Belief Systems. It's not really the affirmation itself that impressed me, but it was the way he began the affirmation. He said the words,

"If you love God say God. But if you connect with Love Spirit or Source, Guides, Angels, Mother Earth, or Universe, then pick your favorite word to start the affirmation. This enhances the affirmation and makes it easier to embrace and believe."

"With God, With Source, With Love, With my Angels, With Mother Earth, With My Higher Self."

Do it now.
Decide on an affirmation and write it down

_____

Now add the words that make you feel the strongest and most loved and write the affirmation again.

With _____, I   am

_____

Now put your hands on your heart and if possible, state the affirmation 10 times out loud. (Or in your mind if you don't want anyone to hear you.) Decide to state your new mantra 10 times twice a day. Notice how you feel adding these words to the affirmation. For me, I feel stronger and more empowered. It also makes it easier for me to believe it's possible for me.

CHAPTER 41

Complex Regional Pain Syndrome (CRPS)
Amanda Wright

Complex Regional Pain Syndrome (CRPS) is a recognized medical condition causing severe, long term
pain. It is usually felt in the limbs of sufferers, and
frequently follows surgery or an injury such as a bone
fracture, with the pain continuing after the injury has
healed and the severity of the pain far exceeding the
pain of the injury.

CRPS is known in medical terms as a functional
pain or neuropathic pain and affects the nerve end-
ings, so that even a light touch of the skin can cause
extreme and severe pain for the sufferer. Other symptoms can include heat or cold sensation, swelling,
rashes, and difficulty moving. Symptoms may change
over time, and may vary from person to person. The
identifiable causes and operation of the condition are
unknown and treatments in traditional medical practice produce unreliable and variable outcomes, and
sometimes may be completely ineffective, especially if
treatment is delayed.

**"Often people come to me when they've tried
everything. Some of them have spent years on**

pain medication. The doctors have told them there is nothing else they can do for them, and they need to live with it." Amanda said.

Amanda uses hypnotherapy to bypass the rational, conscious mind and connect with the client's subconscious mind. In this deeply relaxed state, hypnosis is clinically proven to effectively influence clients' thoughts and behavior at a deeper, subconscious level.

"I find that hypnosis is a good, efficient way to deal with health conditions. I'm dealing with the subconscious mind, coming at the problem from a different direction to traditional medicine," Amanda said.

"I've had very good results working with medical practitioners to support their clients who can no longer achieve results. I've had clients who are not only trying to escape long term chronic pain, but also trying to resolve addiction to pain medication."

Amanda knows the impact that pain and debilitating health conditions can make on career, lifestyle and personal freedom. She has chosen hypnosis as her preferred therapy, because it rapidly achieves significant, lasting and positive results without expensive and ongoing pharmaceutical solutions that may have significant side effects.

Since the 1950s, hypnosis has increasingly gained acceptance as a mainstream medical therapy. Doctors, dentists, psychologists and other medical practitioners are using hypnotherapy, or referring patients to qualified hypnotherapists, to complement existing treatments or assist where no further medical treatment is effective.

"There is a deep mind-body connection that I work with as a hypnotherapist," Amanda said. "The client goes into a deep trance state while still being fully aware of their surroundings, and I am able to access the subconscious mind at that deeper level and filter out the conscious mind.

"There is often an emotional connection between the original event or injury that caused the initial pain, and that is held as a pattern in the mind long after the injury has healed. That is the key to unlocking the pain, and the sub-conscious can release that pattern."

"It has been said that physical pain is the brain's way of protecting the individual from the emotional pain they are afraid to experience. Realizing that can promote immediate progress in many cases."

The first step to recovery, Amanda says, is for the client to actively commit to resolving the condition. This is an important step. Some clients have become so used to living with pain that it has come to define who they are. Visualizing a future life free from pain is essential in engaging their emotions and motivation to begin the changes in their mind and body.

Amanda establishes a deep trance state for the client, allowing the subconscious mind to identify the origins of the condition and the emotional pattern accompanying it, which the conscious mind may be unaware of or hiding. The client enters a calm, peaceful, tranquil state, and the subconscious mind is able to release the pain and set up a future free from pain.

The initial release from pain has a positive influence, as the client is able to accept the effectiveness of hypnotherapy and create positive expectations for a pain free future.

Lauren, a woman in her early 60s, came to see Amanda two and half years after being diagnosed with CRPS. A health care worker at a dementia facility, Lauren injured her knee at work when she slipped in the shower assisting a resident. Her injury required surgery, but Lauren was eager to return to the work she loved, which not only gave her an income but a purpose, making confused and vulnerable elderly people feel loved and cared for. After several month rehabilitation from the workers' compensation injury, Lauren was cleared to return to work although she was still suffering pain and taking medication. Several weeks later she was pulled off her feet by a resident and re-injured the knee, again requiring surgery. Despite severe pain, Lauren wanted to return to work and did not blame anyone for her condition, viewing it as a hazard of the work. However her employers decided she was too high a risk, and she was involuntarily retired from her job. Lauren was very unhappy that her former employers had taken away her choice to work and experienced feelings of powerlessness and lack of control. After many unsuccessful visits to pain specialists who said they could do no more for her,

Lauren came to see Amanda, still in severe pain and on strong medication. After one session she reported her pain had dropped from 7/10 to less than 1/10. Six weeks later Lauren reported that she was still without pain and hadn't taken pain medication since that day. She returned for a second visit which successfully reduced her inflammation and swelling, and was given skills to allow her to move on and manage her condition herself into the future.

Lara, a woman also in her 60s, came to see Amanda after 20 years of consulting specialists to manage crippling spinal pain and CRPS throughout her limbs following a serious car accident. Her condition was so debilitating that she was unable to drive a car or even take public transport, and she was addicted to strong pain killers. She reported that her condition had taken all the joy out of her life, and prevented her from favorite pastimes such as caravanning. The accident had 'squashed the car like a sardine tin' and Lara expressed several times that she felt lucky to be alive, and didn't know how she had survived. She heard about Amanda from a hairdresser, and her husband brought her to an appointment with Amanda despite living at the opposite end of the city. Lara said that despite being skeptical she was 'ready to try anything.' She understood that hypnosis could not fix spinal damage but said that to be rid of the pain would be 'the most amazing thing in my life.' After one session with Amanda, Lara's pain was reduced from 8/10 — although it was sometimes much worse than that — to 0/10. She was free from pain for the first time in

20 years and described the feeling as 'bloody marvelous.' She reported the following day that she had enjoyed the best night's sleep she could ever remember. Although a little pain returned she was very happy with that, had self-hypnosis techniques to help manage her condition, and wanted to return for further treatment after a caravanning holiday.

Hypnotherapy involves no form of diagnosis, medical advice or prescription. The client should have been treated by a medical practitioner and diagnosed with CRPS, and ideally referred to a hypnotherapist for further assistance after a course of treatment. Feedback on the hypnotherapy process is given to the medical practitioner. Typically, two to four hypnotherapy sessions prove effective in alleviating the symptoms of CRPS — frequently eliminating them altogether.

With a corporate background in risk, safety and health, and injury management, Amanda has studied alternative therapies for 25 years. She gained her Master Hypnotherapist qualification from one of Australia's leading hypnotherapy academies in 2018. She specializes in pain elimination, freedom from anxiety, panic attacks and irritable bowel syndrome (IBS) from her studio in Mount Hawthorn, Western Australia.

CHAPTER 42

Unbecome Who You Are Not
Becky Shanks

In the Spring of 2016 I was a practicing clinical hypnotherapist and Reiki practitioner with a profound intuitive understanding of how energy and mind/consciousness create a perceived reality. I began studying a complementary quantum healing technique. This was based upon the human mind's capacity to enter theta — the optimal state for healing and the expanded, creative state of consciousness we each pass through while falling asleep and awakening each day. In this place, the conscious, thinking mind relaxes into a single-pointed focus, the subconscious opens, and anything we can imagine becomes possible.

At that time I started playing a celestite Crystal Tones Alchemy Singing Bowl™, a beautiful blue crystal that attuned me to the realm of the Angels and fostered clearer communication with Highest Self. I began channeling with more and more ease, and quickly learned how to guide busy, stressed minds into theta using my voice, suggestion, intention and crystal singing bowls. I also began to consciously explore the creative power of mind paired with vibration and sound.

Everything is energy. All energy vibrates, and vibrations resonate at unique frequencies — vibrations create sounds, both audible and inaudible.

You might consider the subconscious as a super computer with a hard drive full of files. Sometimes the mind accesses the wrong file folder, or the file held within that folder is corrupt — the program has crashed, and the document needs to be repaired, re-covered, rewritten. Sometimes a virus or malware is introduced, wreaking havoc on the entire system.

It is entirely possible to communicate directly with subconscious, ask it to make the repair, uncross the wires, ground the shorting-circuit, or clear the out-moded programming altogether. Drain ThatPain fosters that communication.

Imagine a conversation that somehow allows you to begin to gently expand beyond limitation, doubt, and even the confines of your physical body. As this con-versation unfolds, you feel safer and safer, comfort-able to move toward and feel whatever has been longing for your careful attention. In choosing to ac-knowledge and accept the information held in emo-tions; in choosing to witness and experience hard feelings, a powerful, subtle process ensues.

An aside: I believe that everything that has ever happened is happening right now. There are parts of us having experiences in the past, parts projecting into the future, parts of us living past lives. The mind uses the information in present emotions to locate res-onant frequencies in other places and spaces.

You know what it's like to be driving along and hear your favorite song on the radio. Without a thought, inkling or direction, you are instantly transported to a moment where you are having the time of your life laughing, dancing, celebrating. You might experience waves of joy, exhilaration associated with the memory — perhaps your heart beats fast, or the experience overwhelms your eyes with tears. You are actually just driving along listening to your favorite song — you have essentially time traveled to meet your younger self and relive the moment.

Drain ThatPain works with the mind's capacity to locate and liberate quantum energy, emotions, thoughts, imprints that had been held captive in the past. Once witnessed, felt, empowered, the stuck energy moves. As dense trapped energies release, your frequency begins to increase, and the brain starts creating an environment for healing within the body.

My practice, *Presents of Mind*, dissolves ego structures and false identities. As we release who we thought we were, who we are begins to shine through; we are Light. Love. Potential Energy. It's as if expanding beyond limited thinking allows the Higher Self to more fully occupy the physical body, as well as the present moment. As we sink deeper and deeper into the Self, cellular memories are activated and released (Yes. Your CELLS have memories, too!), clearing the crystalline structure that is You.

At the same time, every thought we think conditions our cells. Human beings are continuously programming minds, bodies, and auric fields with the frequencies of thoughts and words. We are constantly introducing quantum energy, frequencies, and potentials into our auric fields, as well as re/deprogramming our body-minds with the frequencies of our thoughts and vibration of spoken words.

As old, dense, heavy energy is processed, expressed, and released; as all that no longer serves flows right out — you feel lighter and lighter, brighter and brighter. The frequency of your body literally increases, creating the optimal environment for healing within the body. Latent DNA turns on. Healthy genes expression follows.

Harmony, balance, stasis returns to the entire body-mind system, and the physical body simultaneously begins reflecting the subconscious energetic shifts you have made!

CHAPTER 43

Hypnosis, NLP and Zhineng Qigong "Happiness Operation System"

My name is Isil (pronounced Ichelle) Musluer and I am a Hypnotist and NLP Trainer based in Istanbul, Turkey. I am a licensed trainer of "The Society of NLP™" and Dr.Richard Bandler; the co-inventor of NLP. NLP is short for Neuro-Linguistic Programming, which means programming the mind by using its language.

I have a center in Istanbul where I give NLP Certification trainings with certificates coming directly from Dr. Bandler and I see clients for individual hypnosis and NLP sessions both in-house and online.

At the same time, I am a certified trainer of Zhineng Qigong, which is an integrated system with a complete theory and slow motion meditation practices originating from China. It provides an effective path to take charge of one's physical health and wellbeing. Ultimately it aims to liberate human energy in all its forms and open one's heart to awakening.

In my two chapters I would like to share the story of how I was introduced to these three concepts; what they mean to me and what I learned over the years through them. I would also like to elaborate on their connection to Drain ThatPain work.

First of all, I would like to thank Joanna Cameron for asking me to write a chapter. I was touched and felt honored by her request. Yet at first, I hesitated a bit. I was not sure whether I was the right person to contribute to her book or not? Because after all, in the presence of so many great hypnotists, NLP'ers and Zhineng Qigongers, most of them having 20, 30 or 40+ years of experience, the totality of what I know remains minuscule.

I then considered that so many hypnotists did not know about NLP in depth. Yet, NLP brings very fast and guaranteed shortcuts to predictable results. Likewise, many NLP'ers, do not dive into the depths of hypnosis, but if they do, they may find out that NLP transforms into a magical tool when they combine the two. Zhineng Qigongers on the other hand can utilize hypnosis and NLP very effectively to enhance their work.

So I thought, I might as well be a "Diplomat for Hypnosis, NLP and Zhineng Qigong" and inspire everyone to learn and use all three of them in their lives. This is a novelty in the world and I think there is great potential in their combination.

All these three start from different places, yet they end up on the same road going to the same destination. I think the journey can be faster, safer and more successful if they can be integrated.

I would also like readers of this book and especially the skeptics among them to find some inspiration and validity to research the matter more. Especially after learning how a serious, analytical, scientific person like myself, ended up finding a lot of meaning and potential in this work. Even to the extent that I transformed my entire life and career to make this my full time profession.

I have to add that I consider my current job the most important and the most serious job I have ever had! I give it so much importance and I am so fascinated by it that learning and advancing in it simply becomes a joyful process. Touching hundreds of people's lives in a very positive way seems like a loving spin-off that accompanies my joy of learning. I feel I have the best job in the world.

I had no connection at all in my past with any of these subjects. I was a career diplomat, representing Turkey in countries like France and Azerbaijan. After working for the Ministry of Foreign Affairs for 8 years, I resigned and formed my own foreign trade company. I wanted to work independently where I could be more creative, and I realized this aim. In the following 16+ years, I worked for my own company.

To tell you the truth, if anybody told me in those days that I would become a professional hypnotist and NLP'er one day, I might have simply laughed.

People sometimes say, "I read a book and my whole life changed." Well, this is actually true for me. Because for me, everything started with a book!

The book I refer to is a short transcript of a talk called, "An evening with Richard Bandler: Introduction to NLP." (It is possible to buy it on Amazon in DVD format or you can visit my website to get a download link.) This was a talk given by Dr. Richard Bandler to a group of people where he, quite humorously, explained how he and his co-partner then, John Grinder discovered NLP in the 1970's. Dr. Bandler was talking about hypnosis; how Dr. Milton Erickson, a legendary therapist, was getting extraordinary results with clients using hypnosis, and how he and his co-partner modeled Erickson to draw out the patterns in his unique style and integrate them with NLP.

Reading this surprised me very much. I knew about NLP since the 1990's yet I never realized that it had a connection with hypnosis. I was intrigued! I started to feel a burning desire to learn more.

After some research, I signed up for a hypnosis class. My attitude was very much like signing up for a hobby class. I did not intend to continue more than one training. However, when the class started, my mind was blown away. I did not know that the subconscious was such an influential factor in our lives and 90-95% of what we considered as our conscious choices were under the rule of the subconscious. I learned that hypnosis was a doorway to the subconscious and when changes were made in the limiting subconscious programs, enormous positive changes occurred in people's lives. I was "off to the races" with my desire to learn more. One training followed another. The deeper I went, the greater my pleasure in learning was becoming.

Then the second step in my training started when I signed up for a Neuro Linguistic Programming (NLP) training. NLP is a new and innovative technology that enables practitioners to program the mind, achieve positive and fast results that once were inconceivable.

NLP consists of thousands of techniques that guide practitioners in reaching positive outcomes. NLP believes that human beings are capable of much more than they think possible and views life as a rare and unprecedented opportunity to learn.

With this perspective, NLP seeks out ways to understand and develop new methodologies that can lead individuals to increase their life choices and expand their life satisfaction

When I started my NLP trainings after learning about hypnosis and the subconscious mechanisms, I was once again very positively surprised! NLP was also creating changes in the subconscious just like hypnosis but the steps in NLP were like mathematical formulas. You could follow these formulas and at the end, reach a positive outcome each and every time. NLP was very clear, very easy to apply and worked very fast in getting successful results. NLP worked so beautifully and so effortlessly that exceptional results could be achieved by anyone. They did not have to be a genius to replicate the successful work of people like Milton Erickson. I simply loved it.

I. Musluer

What is also very interesting about NLP is that it works without the need to take the client to deep trance states. Nothing looks mystical, magical, dangerous or unreal about NLP. This frees NLP from all the negative associations of hypnosis, even though it works on the same plane. This gives NLP such a great edge as it opens the doors for getting wider acceptance all around the world. This, in turn, allows NLP to take on a greater role in contributing to humanity. I think this is a very important aspect of NLP.

Now NLP is used in many fields such as education, health, business, politics, art and sports. It assists people to go beyond their limitations, increase their choices, gain exceptional skills and attain success.

While I had all these trainings, I also started applying them on everyone around me. The outcome was shocking! Here I was, an amateur, yet already getting life-changing positive results on people. I started feeling like I found a magic wand, and whoever I touched became empowered.

One day, I entered a children's toy shop to buy something that I could use to represent a magic wand in my sessions. I asked the shop owner whether they had a "magic wand." He replied jokingly that they had wands, but not magic ones. We laughed! Surely, a magic wand doesn't exist. Yet it feels very much like it does if you see people transform before your eyes so easily and effortlessly.

That was the background of my trainings on hypnosis and NLP. I never intended to

be professional. Yet I became one, very fast. Fate seemed to have some plans for me in its pocket.

After hearing me talk about how surprisingly NLP and hypnosis worked, a psychotherapy center's owner asked me if I would like to try it on one of their clients. I said of course! My self-confidence was at peak. I understood the mechanism so well that I did not see any possibility for me to fail.

My first session was with a civil engineer who had a severe flight phobia and who had been having sessions at the therapy center for two years. He was financially well off and had the means to travel anywhere he wanted. Yet, he was unable to go beyond where his car would take him. Our session was wonderful. Everything was flowing. I even noticed that I was automatically integrating the style of Dr. Richard Bandler, whose videos I have watched hundreds of times. It was interesting to realize how the subconscious learned at a deeper scale and put everything into use easily. The outcome of the first session was incredible! A client was freed from his phobia with only one session of NLP. This was extremely surprising and unbelievable for the client and me! I was so confident about getting a positive outcome, even with my first client! I was joyful.

After that first session, relatives and friends of this civil engineer started flooding the therapy center to get an appointment from me. So we agreed with the therapy center that I would go to their center once a week and have sessions with their clients. The other days, I was busy in my foreign trade work.

In almost each and every case, I was getting very positive results. If I told people that I had magical powers, some might have even believed me. Yet, all I did was apply the powerful techniques of NLP that created change in the subconscious programming of the human mind.

I was learning incessantly from every source I could find because this was the most enjoyable subject. I was also gaining practical experience with a huge variety of cases, observing each time which technique generated what type of outcome. The fact that I was an educated and experienced business woman allowed me to gain the respect and support of both the clients and the therapists working at the center.

I was amazed how easily and effectively these techniques brought about changes. In the trainings I learned that the mechanisms were very powerful. Yet, I could never have imagined such amazing results. Dramatic results became so frequent that every time I started a new session, I was sure that the outcome would be extraordinary. Interestingly, every time it was!

These techniques could be applied for not only resolving problems but also for increasing a person's capabilities and choices. In most cases, it is easily possible to transform an average artist, sportsman, businessman or student into an exceptional one. NLP "Modeling" can be used to replicate successful results achieved by others. Creativity, confidence, and health could be improved and all this could be done without the need to make a diagnosis or employ a therapy structure. Therefore NLP is free from issues like wrong diagnosis or incorrect therapy methods. If one technique does not give the desired outcome, another can be applied until the positive outcome is received. Thus it does not attempt to treat anything. It simply re-educates and integrates the conscious and unconscious mind.

I had so many examples of wonderful changes. For example, a neurologist friend's 16 year-old-son who was getting failing grades such as 2 or 3 out of 10 became the brightest kid at school and received the top 60th grade in a nationwide exam a few months later. We met only once and worked for a total of 3 hours. An ambassador friend who smoked for 40 years, flew to Turkey to have an appointment with me and stopped smoking after a few hours of work. A 37-year-old woman, continually trembling and unable to communicate properly, who had to leave school at the age of 12, appeared at her second appointment — free from all the trembling and communication problems. I met with her twice for a total of 4 hours. A stuttering 13-year-old boy, no longer stuttered when we finished our 3-hour session. A 7-year-old girl, wetting her pants every night, stopped doing it after a single one hour session. An alcoholic of 9 years, who requested an appointment to work with me for self-confidence was totally freed from her addiction after 6 hours of work. Now she is even able to drink one or two glasses when she goes out without continuing further.

I. Musluer

All these are not pure coincidences or achieved by indescribable methods. Nor are they magical or meta-physical. They are the outcome of the application of NLP procedures and techniques defined several decades ago. These techniques work, and my work is proof of this. One does not even need to be a therapist to do them, as they do not involve a diagnosis or a treatment procedure. NLP is accepted as an educational process in the world, even though the outcome may be therapeutic.

On the other hand, I wondered why all these methods were not already taught at medical schools. It should not be a choice — I reasoned — it should be an absolute necessity. If it is possible to bring a solution to the problem of a patient by applying some techniques, then why not apply it on a wider scale.

I later realized that it necessitates a total shift in the current point of view towards therapy. Evidently, this is very difficult.

Secondly, it is engraved in the minds of most people that a fast and easy solution to a difficult problem is not possible. This attitude usually prevents the opportunity to check and see whether a claim merits further study or not. I really hope this attitude changes in the near future.

On the other hand, now that I believed that these techniques could bring about absolutely wonderful results and that they should be taught to as many people as possible, I decided to continue my trainings further and become a trainer of this subject. So I contacted "The Society of NLP™" the institution that Dr.

Richard Bandler established. My present trainings were not accepted as valid, as I had to follow their curriculum of training. So I started getting trainings on NLP, from "The Society of NLP™" trainers that came to Turkey from abroad. Once I completed them all, I then went to Dr. Bandler himself, received his trainer trainings in the USA and finally became one of his "Certified International Trainers." This was absolutely a source of pride for me. Now I was able to teach NLP everywhere in the world with a certification coming directly from Dr. Richard Bandler.

Following my return to Turkey, I stopped working in my foreign trade company, transferred the work to my brothers, and I opened a center in a beautiful district of Istanbul called Caddebostan. My office is now situated within five minutes reach of both the fanciest street of Istanbul, and the longest seashore surrounded with parks. Then I embarked on a wonderful new path. Now, I teach all these powerful techniques and I continue to have private sessions with clients. Dramatic outcomes started becoming more frequent and more pronounced. Each and every case teaches me something new and expands my horizon. I call this "the journey within the human Soul," and I consider myself an eternal student in this respect.

I hope many who read these words can also find inspiration to discover the beauty and potential of this work. I cannot stress how wonderful it is to be able to guide people to achieve such important changes and watch them start "shining like stars!" It simply is priceless.

It is possible to work NLP techniques with anyone who desires a change. Yet, there is an absolute necessity for the client to want the change. During the sessions, the client is not a passive recipient of what is given. They are active participants of the techniques. So their cooperation is a must. Otherwise, a positive outcome may not be attainable or may remain less than what can be achieved.

So I made it a principle and priority to work with clients who are resolved to change. Sometimes their family members or friends ask for an appointment. Yet, I make it clear that I need to get confirmation from the client. If the client lacks information or has questions, I respond, and at the end, I always ask, "Do you want the change?" If the reply is not an absolute "YES," I do not consent to work with them.

I tell them that I attach a lot of importance to this work. I work with utmost seriousness and care. I work with the intention to bring about almost magical changes, and I make every effort to reach a solution. So, I say, I absolutely require the same dedication. In fact, with all the clients I work with, I get that dedication which allows me to work with nearly 100 per cent success rates. Such high success rates are fantastic, I think.

Additionally, I also make it clear, that they do not need to believe in NLP or hypnosis in order for us to get successful results. As long as they desire the positive change and cooperate with me, I say that it is possible to work. Nonetheless, I also add that a belief is useful for us, as it may increase the dedication and cooperation of a client.

In this respect, I really feel like a diplomat of hypnosis and NLP. The way I represent and present my work generates interest in people who are unfamiliar with the subject and my personal dedication and seriousness about it attracts respect. The result is a greater audience and an openness towards understanding hypnosis and NLP.

The reason hypnosis and NLP are so effective and transformative is because they make changes in the subconscious. Even a slight positive change in the subconscious can emerge as a miraculous change on the surface.

The subconscious is very interesting. Its communication style is different from the conscious mind and it is very powerful. It controls 90-95% of our lives. Even the majority of choices we think we make with our free will are under the control of the subconscious. When we learn and dive deep into it, it is really frightening to realize how little control we have about ourselves. Yet knowledge is power. If we can learn the language of the subconscious and understand how the mechanism works, then positive behavior changes can begin.

Subconscious is like the most advanced computer that could ever be invented in the world. It controls all the automatic processes of our body, and it can store and process enormous amounts of data. The speed with which it can act is also incomparable with any computer that exists.

So this giant human-computer rules us 95% of the time, and we are hardly aware of it. While doing this, it relies on data that it stored over the years. We call it the "reference system." The reference system shapes the way subconscious works, and this is where the problem arises. 95% of the reference system data is stored when we were very young, within the first 5-7 years of our lives. So for example, if there is a recording in the subconscious, such as "the world is an unsafe place," then this will keep on playing throughout life. Subconscious may then continually seek for a danger that creates this unsafe environment, and the person may be living in a fight or flight mode. Another example might be a recording such as "I am not valuable." If this is what keeps playing in the subconscious, then the person concerned may always be in search of proving that they are valuable, through achieving more success, more beauty, more money, etc. Yet, deep down they can never have satisfaction, as they would still feel unvalued. If one day they lose some of the external sources that they base their value on, like their job success, then the failure they may perceive can be an existential type of failure.

These types of recordings definitely bring a limitation to a person's life. Most of the time, we are unaware of these recordings and their consequences, yet we may feel that we are not completely happy and fulfilled and try to make arguments about why we are like that. Usually, our arguments will have no connection at all with the recording in the reference system. We may feel lonely, unloved, unhappy and unsuccessful, due to a job, a person or a lack of money. Yet we may not realize that the problem actually arises due to a negative reference system recording that we made, for example, when we were 5 years old.

It is possible to learn the mechanism of the subconscious and learn the language with which the subconscious speaks. If we can do this, we then can notice the negative reference system recordings that limit our lives. This would allow us to make important changes.

Imagine changing the "I am not valuable" recording to "I am valuable no matter what I do or how I am. There is no way for me to be not valuable" When we do this, we not only stop the subconscious from controlling our lives, but instead we gain the cooperation of a "supercomputer" in the direction of what we really want.

This whole process makes such a big shift in a person's life that suddenly conflict turns into harmony. Struggle transforms into flow, creativity and health. Success and happiness flourish. The person starts feeling a "deep sense of peace." Generally loneliness disappears — irrespective of whether the person is alone or not. Feelings of anxiety about future or death decline. There may still be problems in a person's life. They might still get angry or sad on occasions, yet the underlying feeling will be happiness and peace.

This is exactly like a summary of what we do. We

can make this shift happen by using the techniques that we have. Hypnosis is like an entrance door to the subconscious, and it is possible to guide clients to make substantial positive changes in the subconscious through hypnosis. On the other hand, NLP also allows practitioners to get fast and successful results by making changes in the subconscious. The difference is NLP generally simplifies and speeds up some of the work we do in the subconscious with hypnosis.

When such a shift happens, the true potential of a person starts emerging. Such a shift also resolves the majority of the conflicts between the conscious and the subconscious minds which actually lay at the core of every problem. When the conflict between these two resolves, conscious and subconscious minds start going in the same direction and much faster than before. It is just like the operating system of our giant human-computer is upgraded to a better one. Computer crashes end and we can function with a speed and efficiency that never existed before. I call this new operating system the "Happiness Operating System."

Everything changes when a person is upgraded to the "Happiness Operating System." Life takes on new colors, and happiness is no longer an end target, but an existing element of life that accompanies everyday. This is also my personal experience after hypnosis and NLP entered my life.

What is more important is that it is possible to upgrade people to the "Happiness Operation System" and quite fast as well. Clients come to me to resolve a debilitating problem or a seemingly unimportant one.

They may even be unaware of what the problem is, yet feel that something is missing in their lives. In all cases, I always work with the intention of the end result of upgrading them to "Happiness Operating System." Surprisingly, almost 90% of the time I achieve this result. I will soon be presenting a protocol on it (which I might name "Protocol on the Happiness Operating System,") where I will set the steps to be followed for other hypnotists and NLP'ers to get the same results.

In a similar manner, most forms of pain and healing follow exactly the same path.They are closely linked to the subconscious. Any change in the subconscious may result in a powerful and dramatic change in a person's life relating to pain and healing. Tormenting, excruciating pain may be eliminated in a matter of hours, and dramatic healing may be achieved. Some of them may seem miraculous, yet they are achievable through the application of the techniques. I have seen it happen many times during my sessions.

For example, once I had a 60-year-old client who was feeling very unhappy due to the anger and hatred she felt towards her mother-in-law. Unfortunately, they were obliged to live together for 30 years. My client was quite embarrassed that she had such strong negative feelings. She had an operation for stomach cancer 6 years ago, and she is in good health now. When I asked her to define the feeling she had in her body at the time she remembered hating her mother-in-law, she told me she felt a solid, rock-type of a feeling gripping her stomach whose color would have been black if it had a color. There are techniques that allow us to find out the underlying reasons why a certain feeling is felt, and that day we found out why she felt the hatred.

Evidently, her subconscious perceived that her mother-in-law was jealous of her when she married and arrived at the house. As the subconscious perceived a possible danger, it set up a protection system for her. The feeling of hatred was a very effective way. Because of the hatred that she felt, she never allowed her mother-in-law to be close to her and the mother-in-law in turn never dared to come close. Yet holding a feeling of hatred for so many years is harmful and in fact my client noticed that she had cancer exactly at the spot where she felt the gripping black rock-like feeling in her stomach.

Then I said to her, "Now that you understand the underlying intention of the subconscious behind creating the feelings of hatred in you, I would like to ask, if your subconscious let's go of producing the feeling of hatred, would it be open to harm; or can you consciously take necessary precautions to protect yourself?" She said, "Of course I can." This may sound ridiculous, yet this is how the subconscious works. After our session that day, my client no longer felt hatred toward her mother-in-law, and the gripping feeling like a black rock disappeared in her stomach.

Our subconscious, while making memory recordings, not only files the images of a memory but also everything associated with it, such as sounds, tastes, smells and their corresponding feelings in our body.

All of them are stored within one file. If one of these elements changes, the file no longer becomes the same and no longer creates the same emotions. Therefore a simple act of changing one of the connections of a file may result in healing a severe phobia, anxiety or a feeling of unworthiness. The memory of the events do not change, yet the emotions that they are tied to change.

This is what happened with my client. It is not possible to say exactly, but I have a sense that she could have had another episode of cancer if she continued to carry that gripping feeling inside her stomach. This is where the secret lies. In order to change the package, and thus change the outcome, sometimes a simple modification in one element that makes up the file of that memory may be sufficient. The underlying program will change automatically.

Pain works in a similar way. The perception of pain, especially when it cannot be linked to a biological problem, may be connected to a memory structure. If the elements connecting to this memory are changed, the total file changes. It may be connected to a desire to punish oneself, for example, or the subconscious may be trying to keep an emotional trauma out of the conscious awareness.

There maybe a message behind the pain or a secondary gain hidden underneath client behavior mechanisms, such as trying to receive love of family members by being in pain. All these may seem far-fetched to the ones who

**don't know the mechanisms,
Yet, professionals already know that they are
true from the language and limiting beliefs of
their clients. In short, if the language of the
subconscious is learned and the mechanisms
understood, it is possible to understand
what the subconscious is doing and
then find a solution.**

Furthermore, the subconscious cannot know the difference between what is imagined and what is real. It also cannot know the difference between past, present, and future. It evaluates everything as happening here and now. When we guide the subconscious to imagine a past trauma and imagine instead experiencing the same event but with a perspective that would resolve the trauma then, the subconscious makes a totally new recording and assumes that the trauma is resolved. This is a fantastic advantage and brings great changes in a person's life.

Likewise, if we can make a client imagine as if though real, the draining of pain away from their body, the subconscious will record it as true, and in fact; what is imagined will be real! Pain will simply be eliminated.

All this can take place when the subconscious is receptive and open. Tactfulness and the elegance of the practitioner make all the difference. NLP allows any practitioner to find the correct roadmap to achieve a successful end result. For Drain ThatPain work, the end result is in fact the total elimination of pain.

As a hypnotist and NLP'er, I can understand the mechanism of Drain That Pain and see why it is successful. Moreover, as a Zhineng Qigong (Wisdom Qigong) practitioner, which is a moving type of meditation and the only form of treatment used in the biggest "Medicineless Hospital" in China, I can also observe numerous similarities between ancient Chinese healing modalities and Joanna's work.

CHAPTER 44

Zhineng Qigong
(Wisdom Qigong)
I. Musluer

I came across Zhineng Qigong approximately 4 years ago when I was researching how to treat cancer with NLP and hypnosis. One of my relatives was diagnosed with cancer, and I wanted to identify the techniques I could use to bring about a change in cancer cases and learn from the experiences of other hypnotists and NLP'ers. I thought that maybe if something is changed in the subconscious, a dramatic change could be attained for healing cancer as well.

While I was researching the subject, I came across a recommendation who advised me to integrate the techniques applied in the "Medicineless Hospital" in China to the NLP work. "If we could do so, it said, our chances of successfully treating cancer would be much greater." I was bewildered! I did not know what they were talking about. So I continued researching. What I found out was mind blowing! Apparently, there was a Zhineng Qigong Center that was established in China in 1988. This center later developed into a training center, healing center, and a scientific research center. The center was called "Huaxia Zhineng Qigong Center" and was referred to as the "Medicineless Hospital." It was closed down in 2001 by the Chinese government. During all these years, more than 350,000 people were treated at this hospital. No medicine or operations were performed. Training and practice of Zhineng Qigong (ZQ) was the only form of treatment. I found out that ZQ was a special form of Qigong.

The history of Qigong dates back thousands of years, and there are numerous different types of Qigong. Some focus on physical strength, some on spiritual development, and some on healing. In almost all forms of Qigong, practitioners learn to quiet their minds and turn inward while they do static or dynamic movements. According to Qigong theories, the daily practice of these movements increase Qi and brings about a free flow of energy which then improves health.

ZQ, however, is a new form of Qigong that was introduced in 1980. It combines physical movements, visualization and a meditative state of mind. It offers a comparably easy methodology to rediscover the inner healing resource within everyone. It is said that it could not only help people improve their intellectual and physical abilities including their health, but also could lead people to develop extrasensory perception abilities, which are considered innate abilities of human beings.

The word "Zhineng" means "wisdom and abilities" and "Qigong," "cultivating life force energy" (Qi=life force energy, gong=work.) ZQ is defined as a life science based on a systematic theory and a methodology that outlines the laws of the Universe, human life, the natural world surrounding it, and society.

The power of Zhineng Qigong comes from Dr. Pang's theories of everything being interrelated in the Universe and the ability to tap into the life-force energy that surrounds us all. ZQ aims to enable everyone to become harmoniously connected with the creative power of the Universe, which is believed to be the origin of love, compassion, and the source of all healing.

The ultimate aim of ZQ, however, is to liberate human energy in all dimensions and open one's heart to awakening.

So I found out that at this "Medicineless Hospital" where ZQ was the only form of treatment, approximately 600 doctors — called teachers — worked and approximately 5000 patients — called students — treated at the hospital at any one time. There were trainings for the students and teachers. Those who healed themselves were so impressed that they usually got trainings and became teachers as well.

When a patient was accepted at the hospital, a file containing their medical records with their blood checks, EKGs, ex-rays, etc. was prepared. Afterward, all patients were released to the common area of the hospital where they collectively practiced ZQ. No medicine or operation was used.

When patients' treatments were completed, their medical files were updated and they were released from the hospital. So all cases were documented, and most of them were published in China. (Some are even available in English too.)

What I found so surprising was the healing rates achieved. In 180 different types of disease, including advanced forms of cancers, the healing rate was 95%. This was the healing rate if all forms of healing were taken into account. If only cases with 100% recovery were taken into account, the figure fell down to 45% but this was still unbelievably high to me. 45% meant that almost 1 out of 2 cases had a 100% recovery rate.

**I could not believe what I was uncovering.
It seemed too good to be true.
So I continued researching.**

I learned that the hospital was initiated by a doctor of both Chinese and Western medicine, named Dr. Pang Ming. He was a Grandmaster of Qigong and a very prolific writer who wrote over a dozen books. He was born in 1940 and grew up in a family where Qigong was practiced regularly; so he was familiar with its positive effects on people.

Studying Qigong under 19 different Grandmasters,

he became a Grandmaster himself. When he became a medical doctor, he was also researching faster and more powerful ways to help his patients. Finally, in 1980 he introduced a new form of Qigong called "Zhineng (wisdom) Qigong" by combining all of his trainings. He then started publishing his theories.

Now Dr. Pang is retired and he focuses on his research and writing books. Whilst being retired he continues to contribute to his society and to Zhineng Qigong. He lives in perfect health and on June 17, 2018, he was appointed Professor of Jiangxi University of Traditional Chinese Medicine.

Dr. Pang Ming's theories expressed his understanding about the Universe and human beings. They were based on both ancient insights and modern scientific knowledge, and they merged the essence of various Qigong styles. Daoist, Buddhist, Confucian, medical Qigong, folk Qigong, and martial arts were all merged with contemporary medicine, science and philosophy. In fact, Zhineng Qigong became the first Qigong type in China that had a fully integrated theory.

Dr. Pang initially intended to teach his findings. Later, however, he decided to form a research center and start applying his findings without necessarily trying to convince anybody of the validity of his arguments. Apparently, contrary to what Westerners assume, even in China there are millions that are unaware of Qi. This research center was actually the "Medicineless Hospital" we refer to. Chinese people never called it a hospital. It was Westerners who gave this name to it.

When I read about all this, I was fascinated. I wanted to learn more, but there was hardly anybody who knew about ZQ near me. Later I found a man who had gone to China for training. I flew to where he was living and received an introductory training from him. This allowed me to understand the concept of Qigong and start applying the practices. From then on, I started practicing every day. I liked the soft flowing movements of Qigong very much. I found them very clever as well. Because while doing the slow flowing movements with the hands and the body, and concentrating on imagining to collect Qi from the surroundings, one was automatically entering into a calm trance-like state. In fact this allowed an easy way to control the mind, which normally is very difficult to realize.

While I practiced, I also started reading extensively. There are a number of books available on Amazon on ZQ. Within 3 months I read almost all of them. Discovery of the theory was something beyond my imagination.Through the theories, I got a better idea of why healing occurred. It fascinated me.

While I continued to practice an hour every day, I started feeling the Qi in a very pronounced way. I could sense the energy movement easily. Of course, I have to say that ZQ is not like hypnosis and NLP. Hypnosis and NLP consist of techniques that are much more scientific compared to ZQ. ZQ has a very precise and consistent way of looking at things; yet much of its arguments await scientific recognition. This however, does not decrease the importance or validity of its arguments, in my eyes.

In fact ZQ has a very wide scope to explain the world around us. Subjects like how Qi mechanism and energies work, how healing occurs, how extraordinary sensory capabilities and their linkage with creating healing develop are fascinating for me. Learning about it was a real stretch for my mind and I felt like I was reading a science fiction book at times.

I also think that learning about a different perspective is a very good thing. Because in the West, we have several problems that cannot be resolved with our current perspective. Healing cancer is one of them. So we need to gain the ability to look at issues from different angles. In China for thousands of years, the Qi mechanism was believed to be closely aligned with healing. So, I think ZQ theories merit further study. We can find out how we can learn them in order to improve our lives in general.

Apart from all these theories, which were fascinating to read, I was enjoying immensely the slow motion practices. They brought clarity and focus to my mind and a general sense of calm to my presence. Surprisingly, the ZQ theories on healing started contributing to my hypnosis and NLP work as well. After getting some clues about why healing occurred in ZQ, and considering that "Qigong State" was a trance-like state, I started using them in my sessions and ZQ became a very rewarding way to achieve results!

In ZQ, the belief is that Qi flows wherever the mind focuses. They believe that all problems and diseases occur because of an insufficient amount of Qi or a blockage in its flow. Thus, I guide my clients during our sessions to imagine sweeping their body with a wonderful flow of energy. It not only benefits them to concentrate and relax but also is in alignment with Qigong healing theories. I am not sure which one heals, but the end result we get is usually positive. That is what I target.

I learned while studying Qigong, that pain can sometimes be interpreted as a call for more resources from the body. Every organ and every part of the body has a function. Whenever there is something wrong with an organ and if it needs more resources from the body, pain is one of the ways it asks for more resources. According to Qigong mechanisms, pain attracts a person's attention and so their mind is focused on the area that produces pain. Therefore Qi starts flowing to that region, which in turn starts healing. Yet there is, of course, a prerequisite. Positive intentions and positive expectation should accompany the focus.

If we assume that the pain is actually a way to ask for more attention through which the life-force energy starts flowing, and if the Qi starts flowing to the organ when the person focuses their mind; then my knowledge of subconscious mechanisms tells me that it may be possible to stop the subconscious from producing this pain if the outcome can be consciously produced by the person. Therefore, I think if a person suffering from chronic pain could imagine healing energies flowing into the organ that needs healing, then the subconscious may simply stop producing the pain. Just like the case of my client who hated her mother-in-law, once the subconscious understands that the person can consciously do what it intends to do by generating pain, then there maybe no reason for the subconscious to continue producing the pain.

We are not sure whether pain is really a cry for more attention or whether focusing the mind can really direct healing energies to the organ or not. Yet your imagination is real for the subconscious, and if it can produce a positive result, then irrespective of whether the arguments are true or not, we can consider the technique is valid. So I think the Qigong point of view in relation to pain may be worth considering.

I am in no position to validate whether the theories of Qigong are true or not. Scientists should carry out studies, review the already available ones in China and publish their findings. Until then, everyone needs to make their own decision on how appealing they find the theories. To me, they seem quite appealing, and I believe that most of them are true. I see evidence of it all the time. However, I can say one thing for certain. Practicing and learning Qigong enriched my life!

Usually many types of meditative work end up taking the form of a new age religion, and they start requiring devotion. I personally do not like this. What I like about ZQ is that it does not transform into a religion. It purely limits itself to energy mechanism and how we can improve our lives in this world. So I am very happy about ZQ.

I started advancing in Qigong, learning from numerous masters and participating in international classes. Finally, I decided to take a trainer's training with a Chinese Master. I recently completed it. It was a long path, and I learned so much. The structure of energy pathways, how Qi can penetrate organs, how Chinese medicine functions, how Qigong differs from Chinese medicine, how healing happens and what type of healing modalities exist? What makes ZQ different and more powerful than any other form of Qigong and how all these techniques should be taught to students were among the subjects we learned. In fact, my awareness expanded.

Qigong enhanced my NLP trainings as well. In the NLP Practitioner Certification Trainings that I give, I started using the "Qi field teaching mechanism" that Dr. Pang explains in his theories. NLP Certification Training is already a very special training. It employs advanced subconscious learning mechanisms that are taught to us by Dr. Richard Bandler. Yet adding the ZQ Qi field teaching mechanism into it made it much more powerful I believe. I do not necessarily share it with students, as it is not something verbal, yet I observe that they find the training much more flowing and powerful, and they learn at a deeper level.

So in summary, I would like to jot down some of the points I learned about ZQ that might inspire readers:

1. According to ZQ how you use your mind and how you think is extraordinarily important. The energy of the mind is special they say, and it is called Yiyuanti.

2. In order for the mind's energy to create transformation and physical change, it needs to be relaxed, calm and empty. It should also have a sense of com-

plete unity with the whole Universe. When this is attained pure consciousness, the true self or, in other words, the Yiyuanti state emerges.

3. Movement is essential for a healthy body.

4. Qigong movements lead a person to concentrate inside. This allows the Qi to accumulate, flow and increase inside.

5. Every movement, like a simple walk, can be considered Qigong if the attention of the mind is drawn inside the body.

6. All sicknesses are caused by disharmony in the circulation of Qi or insufficient Qi in the body.

7. Emotional imbalances and strong negative emotions create imbalances in the flow of Qi.

8. There is no need to concentrate on what the sickness is. If the harmonization of the Qi flow in the body is targeted, healing will occur in all diseases.

9. Zhineng Qigong uses a Qi field to create powerful healing. This is different from other forms of Qigong.

10. Collectively practicing creates a greater impact.

11. When Qi starts flowing harmoniously, positive information/ instruction should be given (like planting a seed) in order to start healing. This can be words like "already healed" or "healthy." Not the process but the end result should be targeted.

12. If bodily Qi increases, then how you use the mind becomes more important as it will create physical change much more powerfully. If the mind cannot be controlled and if negative thought patterns emerge, then increased Qi can be destructive to the body and the mind. It can lead to serious problems and even to

death. So progress should be done in a controlled and careful manner.

13. To define this process, they say that Qi is like a sharp knife. It can heal, but it can also harm. This should not be forgotten.

14. When an illness is being healed in the body, usually a reaction occurs which seems as if the sickness has been aggravated. This is called Qi reaction. Teachers advise to disregard this reaction and continue the practice. (I was incredibly surprised to experience strong Qi reactions I was exposed to as I progressed in my practices.)

15. There are 6 levels in ZQ. Three of them are publicly available. Level 1 contains two different sets. (I spent one year practicing each.)

16. Collecting virtue (Dao) is an essential element of Zhineng Qigong.

Spiritual awakening, development of extrasensory abilities are all linked with this. No matter how advanced a person is in the practices, if the virtue is not present, he/she cannot really attain a stage where powerful healing is created.

17. ZQ uses imagination for healing and guiding Qi. Imagination should take place in the form of an "empty but not empty state" as described by ZQ. This means that the imagination should be relaxed, unat-

tached and carefree. Forcefully trying to visualize the healed state is not a correct manner.

18. There is also a foundation state of ZQ, called the true heart state (which I am practicing right now), where there is almost no need to use the mind actively. Complete silence can be attained for long durations, and a sense of oneness and unity reigns. Healing at this stage starts occurring all by itself. (The experience seems to resemble the Ultra Depth hypnosis state where spontaneous healings are recorded without any instruction given to the subconscious.)

19. Love and a sense of happiness are extraordinarily important. Even if a sick person cannot do the practices or use their mind actively, if they lose themselves in the moment with a feeling of joy and happiness, then healing starts. This is as important, if not more important, than the active imagination of the healed state.

20. Healing should not be considered as a struggle. Terminology like "fighting cancer" is absolutely wrong according to Qigong.

21. When I asked a very advanced Qigong master how they healed people and how they used their minds, he said that they did not try to heal people but instead they tried to heal themselves. I asked what he meant by it, and he said that they were trying to restitute themselves to their "true self," and along the way, healing occurred in others. It seems that the true self-state (which is also called the "real heart state") recognizes that everyone and everything is connected. There is an

intelligent side that knows already what is required, and healing automatically finds its expression.

Dr. Pang Ming says: "Cultivating one's Qi is not the most fundamental pursuit; cultivating one's spirit (pure mind) and conscience is! Mastery of life is really achieved through mastery of consciousness."

The above is only a small portion of what exists in ZQ. I listed the points according to my understanding. So please be aware that I may be wrong or my views may change. I no longer think the way I did a year ago on some points, for example. So I recommend you, use my notes loosely and do not interpret them as absolute facts.

As I said earlier, there is a lot that hypnosis, NLP and ZQ can contribute to each other. NLP works like a magical tool when it is accompanied with a deep knowledge of hypnosis. Hypnosis without NLP, l think, simply omits a very strong, quick and guaranteed tool for getting results. Zhineng Qigong, on the other hand, is a total shift of paradigm in respect to healing and the capabilities of human beings in general.

As to how hypnosis and NLP knowledge may contribute to Zhineng Qigong, I think quite a lot can be found. In Zhineng Qigong, when people practice and stay in a "Qigong state" a healing environment occurs for the body. Yet it is not possible to be in a Qigong state constantly. All the other times, the subconscious broadcasting system (reference system) continues. NLP and hypnosis provide tools to make shifts in this broadcasting system. Qigong says strong negative emotions lead to disease. If recordings on these negative emotions can be changed by NLP and hypnosis, it will be like removing the dirt that blocks the road. The journey of healing with ZQ can be faster this way.

Anchoring is a very powerful tool for replicating positive states in hypnosis and NLP. This can easily be integrated into the work of ZQ. This way, deeper Qigong states can be accessible every time and very quickly.

Another possible area of contribution is that for a beginner, it requires quite some time and experience to attain a Qigong state that will be beneficial for healing. The Qigong state is almost exactly like a trance state. We, hypnotists and NLP'ers, can get our clients to deep trance states immediately without requiring them to have prior experience. This mechanism can be used powerfully by Zhineng Qigong to attain deep Qigong states immediately with new practitioners.

I would like to recommend that you research and read about hypnosis, NLP and ZQ. (Please check my website for guidance on where to start. I will be uploading links.) You can choose to integrate as much as you want into your lives. They all enriched my life in many ways, and I am sure they will enrich yours too. Remember 95% of your lives are controlled by the subconscious. Subconscious is a mystery. The more we bring back to the surface, the more we learn about it and control it, the better we can be at mastering our lives.

If you can, I highly recommend you to get trainings as well. I really do not know any other thing that can help someone faster than hypnosis and NLP. It changes everything. I never intended to be a professional, as you know, yet I became one after seeing what an important contribution it could make to people in general. Now I simply love it.

However, I need to point out that you do not need to be a professional to learn hypnosis and NLP. Once you learn, it will start enhancing your life in a very positive way. You can be a more effective mother raising happier children, a more successful sales person, an empowered leader or an exceptional creative artist. Not only for yourself but you also can start contributing to everyone around you in a very positive way. It is like learning the "user manual for humans beings." For me, it felt like a veil was lifted from my eyes. I could understand many things that seemed incomprehensible before. So I believe you can do the same too.

But, even if you do not get trainings, I advise you to find a way to shift to the "Happiness Operating System" mode by getting sessions. Do you still use the DOS operating system on your computer? I guess not! Why then continue using an outdated system on your mind's computer? It is slowing you down and draining your energy. Upgrade to the advanced "Happiness Operating System!" It is possible. Although the degree of change may vary, it will still be much better than before. So learn it! Learn to do it with others! It is possible! Contact me if you need guidance.

By the way, if you start learning or practicing any of these three concepts after reading my chapters, please share your story with me. I would love to learn about it and follow you to observe how it will enhance your life.

I used to attribute the successes I achieved in my sessions as purely due to techniques, and I always said there was nothing magical about them. I still say so. Yet, after learning ZQ, I wonder! Could there be something beyond that contributes to our positive outcomes? Maybe! I don't know. I target the outcome, and if, as the Chinese say, there is some magic in everything, all the better!

I observe that Drain ThatPain has many things in common with Zhineng Qigong. Setting up intention, creating a feeling of flow (Qi regulation) and imagination of directing energies to the body (working with Qi field) are some of them. Joanna Cameron combines all the powerful mechanisms of hypnosis, NLP, and ZQ into an elegant style. I believe that she creates magic around us and makes lives better and much more beautiful with her work.

ZQ achieved a healing rate of 95% among 350,000 people in China. Why not do the same with Drain ThatPain! I am sure it will! I am now enthusiastically waiting to see the principles of Drain ThatPain applied around the world and hear about the millions of people who have released chronic pain for good!

I.Musluer
www.isilmusluer.com
info2@isilmusluer.com

We thank you for reading our book and hope that you find comfort, inspiration and guidance for a pain free life. If we have inspired you, please show your gratitude by writing a book review on Amazon, or giving this book to someone in pain.

Make a decision to live the life of your Soul's highest intention! Join us as we bring heaven to earth. Drain ThatPain is active on social media and uses the following hashtags #drainthatpain #painelimination #lovingintention #bringheaventoearth

At the time of this book publication, the *Drain That-Pain* documentary is not in general distribution. It is available for private screenings with Joanna Cameron for group events. Joanna will show the film and work with the audience afterwards to facilitate pain elimination. Schedule your event by contacting Doretta Pugh Osburn, Joanna's agent in Nashville for the cost and conditions. Email: Doretta.Osburn@gmail.com

Acknowledgements

I'm so grateful to Ian, Elizabeth and Shirley Cameron, my husband Harvey, and daughter, Chelsea. Thank You Angela Newton Plowman, my childhood friend along with my Shawford family, who's home has been my home for as long as I can remember.

Thank you too Nikola Tesla, Robin Williams, Tad James, Jim Ward, Dr. John Sarno, Mary Lanaras, the Splash Girls, Mike Stryker, Darren Williams, Shanah Zigler, Andrew Rosario, Gabriel Redding, Steve Roehm, Doretta Pugh Osburn, Amanda Dobra Hope, Bill Bengston, Rupert Sheldrake, Andrew Scudder, Abbe Lyle, Carl Klunk, Eden Brown, Richard Boyd, Jason Nobby Morgan, Shelly Rose, Carolee Followill, Jenny Anne Sullivan, Dr. Stephen Reisman, Dan and Myla Champ, Leslie Simpson, Gayle Sheeks, Leigh Meadows, Jeanne Epp, Denise Pineo, Margery McGrath, Amber Rose Cox, Alan Barsky, Jaime Feldman and Pam Holmes.

CHAPTER 46

Drain ThatPain Book and Documentary Contributors

• Joanna Cameron - DrainThatPain, based in the US is a holistic energy technique for chronic pain elimination. On Facebook @painelimination, DrainThatPain Training. On Twitter @DrainThatPain. On Instagram @DrainThatPain. Get your Skype, Zoom or FB Messenger appointment now. Online and groupTrainings. www.drainthatpain.com www.amazon.com/author/joannacameron

• Helen Mitas – International Hypnotist, Author, Teacher, Leader – who empowers, educates and inspires Hypnotherapists to make the greatest impact in the lives of their clients. All trainings. Author of *Mindset Dominance* www.helenmitas.com, www.amazon.com/author/helenmitas

• Becky Willoughby – Psychic Consultant, Medical Intuitive and Physical/Emotional Pain Elimination, based in the UK. Author – *Switch on Your Psychic.* All trainings www.beckywilloughby.co.uk

• Randi Light, MS – Dynamic Peak Performance Coach, Hypnosis Instructor, Healer, Author of The Essential 4 for Physical and

Emotional Pain Elimination. Online and group trainings. Based in the US. www.randilight.org, www.amazon.com/author/randilight

- Jim Ward - Author. America's greatest fiction storyteller. Author of *Irish Luck, Indian Island, Jaguar Jungle, Wicked Habits,* and *Weather War.* https://www.facebook.com/wardjim52, email, JimWard50@aol.com, www.amazon.com/author/jimwardpoet

- Dominique Shipstone – The Mind Coach based in the UK. Founder. Hypnotherapist. Online and group trainings. www.tmc-therapy.com

- I. Musluer, based in Istanbul, Turkey. Hypnotist, International Trainer of NLP (Licensed by "The Society of NLP™" & Dr. Richard Bandler) Zhineng Qigong Trainer. Online sessions and trainings, www.isilmusluer.com

- Carol Robertson, PhD, based in Edinburgh, Scotland. Havening. www.psychosensoryacademy.com, www.haveningtrainings.com www.amazon.com/author/carolrobertsonphd

- Amanda Dobra Hope based in the US. Author, Speaker, Holistic Healer. Online and group trainings. www.itsasyoulikeit.com https://www.amazon.com/Amanda-Dobra-Hope/e/B01M3Z0UD0

- Raye Carr based in the US. Clinical Hypnotherapist/Founder. Online and group trainings. www.rayecarrhypnotherapy.com

- Becky Shanks based in the US. Alchemical Hypnotherapist and Theta Healer. Online and group trainings www.presentsofmindhypnosis.com

- Benetta Wainman, based in Melbourne, Australia. Founder. Online and group trainings www.roadtosuccesshypnotherapy.com.au/services

- Amanda Wright, based in Perth, Australia. Founder. Online and group trainings. CRPS and IBS. www.amandawright.com.au

- Hillary Evans, based in the US. Founder. Online and group trainings www.truehypnosis.com

- Christopher Holden, based in the US. Founder. All trainings. www.hyperionhypnosis.com

- Neota Tinkler, based in British Columbia, Canada, Founder. Online and group trainings. www.en-trance.ca

- Dr. Kristi Judy – based in the US. Online and group trainings. – 1-800-541-9928. www.AcademyForLifeEmpowerment.com

- Peggy Bonfield, based in the US. Founder. Online and group trainings. www.Peggybonfield.wix.com

- Edward Philippe based in the US. Founder. Online and group trainings. www.EdwardPhilipp.com

- Christina Olin, based in the US. Founder.

Online and group trainings.
www.thoughtwaveshypnotherapy.com

• Carol Henderson, based in the US. Founder. Online and group trainings.
www.newdayhypno.com

• Dr. Stephen L. Reisman, based in Brentwood, TN. www.mindbodymedicalcenter.com

CHAPTER 47

Pain Eliminators

- Joanna Cameron – DrainThatPain based in the US is a holistic energy technique for chronic pain elimination. On Facebook @painelimination, DrainThatPain Training. On Twitter @DrainThatPain. On Instagram @DrainThatPain. Get your Skype, Zoom or FB Messenger appointment now. Online and groupTrainings. www.drainthatpain.com, www.amazon.com/author/joannacameron

- Steven Blake - OldPain2Go based in the UK. Founder. Trainers and practitioners worldwide. www.oldpain2go.com

- Freddy Jacquin - "The Arrow" based in the UK. Founder. Online and group trainings. www.freddyjacquin.com

- Becky Willoughby – Psychic Consultant, Medical Intuitive and Physical/Emotional Pain Elimination, based in the UK. Author – *Switch on Your Psychic.* All trainings www.beckywilloughby.co.uk

- Martin Rothery – Rapid pain elimination therapy based in the UK. Founder. Online and group trainings. Sanomentologist www.rapidpaineliminationtherapy.com

- Karen Ferris Therapy Solutions based in the UK. Online and group trainings. www.karenferristherapysolution.co.uk

- Dominique Shipstone – The Mind Coach based in the UK. Founder. Hypnotherapist. Online and group trainings. www.tmc-therapy.com

- Stephen Daly – SDMindMatters based in the UK. Hypnotherapist. Reiki Master. Online and group trainings. www.sdmindmatters.com

- Beryl Comar based in Dubai – author of the ground-breaking book *HypnoDontics* – using hypnosis in dentistry. Trainings. www.berylcomar.com. and www.hypnodonticsworld.com

- I. Musluer based in Istanbul, Turkey. Hypnotist, International Trainer of NLP (Licensed by "The Society of NLP™" & Dr. Richard Bandler) Zhineng Qigong Trainer. Online sessions and trainings, www.isilmusluer.com

- Marcel Borst, based in Amsterdam, the Netherlands. Founder. Online and group trainings. www.ikleefwel.nl, www.drainthatpainholland.nl

- Neota Tinkler, based in British Columbia, Canada, Founder. Online and group trainings. www.en-trance.ca

- Freja Norden, based in Toronto, Canada. Founder. Online and group trainings. www.makelovebetter.ca

- Vivienne Filiatreault, based in Ottawa, Canada. Founder. Specializing in trauma, anxiety. Hypnotherapist. www.viviennefiliatreault.com, www.Richconnections.ca

- Randi Light, MS – Dynamic Peak Performance Coach, Hypnosis Instructor, Healer, Author of *The Essential 4 for Physical and Emotional Pain-elimination.* Online and group trainings. Based in the US. www.randilight.org, www.amazon.com/author/randilight

- Alan Barsky, based in the US. Online and group trainings. www.hypnotherapy-marin.com

- Amanda Dobra Hope based in the US. Author, Speaker, Holistic Healer. Online and group trainings. www.itsasyoulikeit.com https://www.amazon.com/Amanda-Dobra-Hope/e/B01M3Z0UD0

- Scott Schmaren, based in the US. Founder. Online and group trainings www.UltimateVisionaryMind.com

- Stephanie C. Conkle based in the US. Founder. Online and group trainings. Profound Somnambulism Protocol, www.clearliferesults.com, www.stephanieconkle.com

- Raye Carr based in the US. Clinical Hypnotherapist/Founder. Online and group trainings. www.rayecarrhypnotherapy.com

- Becky Shanks based in the US. Alchemical

Hypnotherapist and Theta Healer. Online and group trainings www.presentsofmindhypnosis.com

- Christopher Holden, based in the US. Founder. All trainings. www.hyperionhypnosis.com

- Sandra Bemis based in the US. Founder. Hypnotist, Trainer. Online and group trainings. www.wholehealthhypnosis.com

- Amber Rose Cox, based in the US. Founder. Online and group trainings www.Mainehypnosiscenter.com

- Silvia Anne Milone-Martin, based in the US. Author. Founder. Online and Group trainings. www.tinytrancer.com, http://www.facebook.com/sam4228

- Dr. Kristi Judy based in the US. Online and group trainings. – 1-800-541-9928. www.AcademyForLifeEmpowerment.com

- Theresa Micheletti based in the US. Online and group trainings. Spiritual and Clinical Hypnosis www.GnosticLightKeepers.com, www.PremierHypnosisTrainingCenter.com

- Michelle Braun based in the US. Founder. Online and group trainings. www.Manifestintent.com

- Edward Philippe based in the US. Founder. Online and group trainings. www.EdwardPhilipp.com

- Christina Olin, based in the US. Founder. Online and group trainings. www.thoughtwaveshypnotherapy.com

- Peggy Bonfield, based in the US. Founder. Online and group trainings. www.Peggybonfield.wix.com

- Josh Peters, based in the US. Founder. Online and group trainings www.integratedhypnosis.com

- Carol Henderson, based in the US. Founder. Online and group trainings. www.newdayhypno.com

- Randi Light, based in the US. Founder - Essential 4. Peak-Performance Coach. Online and group trainings. www.randilight.org

- Hillary Evans, based in the US. Founder. Online and group trainings www.truehypnosis.com

- Val Cook, based in the US. Founder. Online and group trainings www.valcook.net

- Debra Stone McNab, based in the US. Founder. Online and group trainings www.studiohypnosis.com

- Helen Mitas, based in Melbourne, Australia. Founder of the thriving Hynofit clinic, helping thousands with addictions, depression, anxiety and chronic pain. Online and group trainings. Author of *Mindset Dominance*   www.hypnofit.com.au, www.helenmitas.com

www.amazon.com/author/helenmitas

• Benetta Wainman, based in Melbourne, Australia. Founder. Online and group trainings www.roadtosuccesshypnotherapy.com.au/services

• Jan Davidson, based in Melbourne, Australia. Founder. Weight loss. Online and group trainings. www.hypnohealing.com.au

• Teresa Mullins, based in Melbourne, Australia, Founder. Online and group trainings. https://www.facebook.com/teresa.mullins.5099

• Karen Bradford, based in Melbourne, Australia. Founder. Online and Group Trainings. www.perfectlybalancedlife.com.au

• Annie Walker, based in New South Wales. Founder. Online and group trainings. www.bathursthypnotherapy.com.au

• Andrew George Pietruska, based in Adelaide, South Australia. Founder. Online and group trainings. www.facebook.com/andrew.pietruszka

• Amanda Wright, based in Perth, Australia. Founder. Online and group trainings. CRPS and IBS. www.amandawright.com.au

• Nikki Taylor, based in Perth, Australia. Founder. DrainThatPain Trainer. Online and group trainings. www.hypnosissolutionswa.com

• Rebecca Privilege, based in Perth, Australia. Founder. Online trainings and group trainings www.rebeccaprivilege.com

- Craig Denny, based in Newcastle, Australia. Founder. Online and group trainings.
www.drainthatpainnewcastle.com.au

- Carol Robertson, PhD, based in Edinburgh, Scotland. Havening.
www.psychosensoryacademy.com,
www.haveningtrainings.com
www.amazon.com/author/carolrobertsonphd

- Rhona Wands (Rhona-Bee) Founder in Scotland. All trainings.
www.facebook.com/titchyboo1111
Email rhonawands@hotmail.com

- Andileeb Ahmed, based in the UK. Founder. Online and group trainings.
www.aurorahypnoclinic.com

- Kim Thomas, based in the UK. Founder. Online and group trainings.
www.anewyoutherapy.co.uk

- Nina Crawley, located in the U.K. Online and group trainings
www.kent-hypnotherapy-practice.co.uk

CHAPTER 48
Further Reading

• Bach, Richard, *Illusions: The Adventures of a Reluctant Messiah*, Delacorte Press 1977.

• Bandler, Richard and Morgan, Mark, 2009. *Get the Life you want. The Secrets to Quick and Lasting Life Change using Neuro-Linguistic Programming* by Richard Bandler, Mark Morgann, et al. Dec 23, 2009. Audible

• Bandler, Richard. *Using Your Brain for a Change*. Moab, Utah: Real People Press, 1985

• Bengston, William, PhD. *The Energy Cure - Unlocking the Mystery of Hands-On Healing*. Sounds True, Inc. 2010

• Braud, W and Schlitz, M.J. "Consciousness interactions with remote biological systems: anomalous intentionality effects." Subtle Energies, 1991; 2(1): 1-46. www.aipro.info/drive/File/224.pdf

• Chopra, Deepak. *The Seven Spiritual Laws of Success*. Amber - Allen Publishing, San Rafael Publishing, 1994

• Rumi Da, spiritual guide. Authority on the use of crystals in healing and Awakening! www.vogelcrystals.net

• Dooley, Mike. *Infinite Possibilities. The Art of Living Your Dreams*. Simon & Schuster. 2009

• Dyer, Wayne W. *Inspiration. Your Ultimate Calling*. Hay House, Inc. 2006

• Dyer, Wayne W. *The Power of Intention. Learning to Co-create Your World Your Way*. Hay House, Inc. 2004

• Emoto, Masaru. *The Hidden Messages in Water*. Beyond Words Publishing, Inc. 2001

• Feinstein, David, Donna Eden, Gary Craig. *The Promise of Energy Psychology*. New York: Penguin 2005

• Gordon, Richard. Quant*um-Touch:The Power to Heal:* North Atlantic Books, Berkeley, CA. 1999

• Goswami, Amit. *The Quantum Doctor*, Charlottesville, VA: Hampton Roads Publishing Company Inc., 2004

• Hay, Louise. *Heal Your Body*. Hay House 1984

• James, Tad, and Wyatt Woodsman. *Time Line Therapy™ and the Basis of Personality*, Capitola, CA: Meta Publications, 1988

• Levine, Peter A, PhD and Maggie Phillips, PhD. *Freedom from Pain*, Sounds True, Inc. Boulder, Co. 2012

- Lipton, Bruce. *The Biology of Belief.* Santa Rosa, CA: Mountain of Love, Elite Books, 2005

- Ming, Dr. Pang. T*he Methods of Zhineng Qigong Science (Volume 1).* Patricia Fraser; 1 edition. 2013

- Ruiz, Don Miguel. *The Four Agreements.* Amber-Allen Publishing, 1997

- Sarno, John. *The Divided Mind! The Epidemic of Mind/Body Disorders* Harper Collins, 2009

- Sarno, John. *Healing Back Pain: Mind Body Connection.* New York: Warner Books, 1991

- Schechter, David, M.D. *Think Away Your Pain. Your Brain is the Solution to Your Pain.* MindBody Publications 2014

- Virtue, Doreen. *Chakra Clearing.* Carson, CA: Hay House, 1994

- Willoughby, Becky. *Switch On Your Psychic. The Simple Way to Develop Your Intuition.* HypnoticArts.com, 2017

Printed in Great Britain
by Amazon